Beginners ESL Lesson Plans Book 2

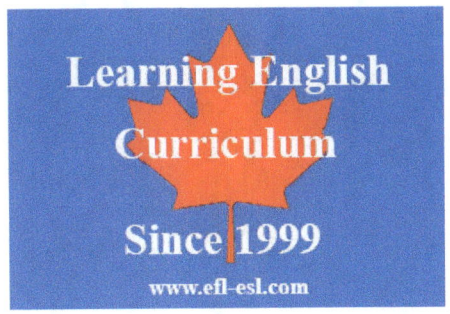

Learning English Curriculum

Copyright © 2023 ALL RIGHTS RESERVED.

You are permitted to print or photocopy as many copies as you need for your school. Online distribution is not permitted. Please contact us if you wish to teach online.

Re-Sales is not permitted.

Notice: Learning English Curriculum makes every reasonable effort to obtain from reliable sources accurate, complete, and timely information about the tests covered in this book. Nevertheless, changes can be made in the tests or the administration of the tests at any time and Learning English Curriculum makes no representation or warranty, either expressed or implied as to the accuracy, timeliness, or completeness of the information contained in this book. Learning English Curriculum make no representations or warranties of any kind, express or implied, about the completeness, accuracy, reliability, suitability or availability with respect to the information contained in this document for any purpose. Any reliance you place on such information is therefore strictly at your own risk.

The author(s) shall not be liable for any loss incurred as a consequence of the use and application, directly or indirectly, of any information presented in this work. Sold with the understanding, the author is not engaged in rendering professional services or advice. If advice or expert assistance is required, the services of a competent professional should be sought.

Published by:
Learning English Curriculum

ISBN 9781772454147

Visit us on the Web at
https://www.efl-esl.com

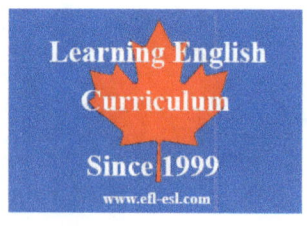

Learning English Curriculum
Victoria, B.C. Canada
E-mail: **info@efl-esl.com**

TEACHING PHILOSOPHY

Our teaching philosophy means that the students and teachers can combine fun and learning, while communicating in English. This is a structured approach, meaning that each new concept is mastered in a conversational English environment before another is introduced. During the past decade, research has shown that the students learn more effectively if the teaching of grammar is integrated with a communicative approach to the learning of the English language.

This program is written for students 13 years and older. We introduce the basic tenses and other structures in a logical sequence, integrating them with light hearted activities that provide practice in a conversational setting. The combination achieved in our curriculum has proved to be popular with the students and successful in achieving its goals.

TIMING AND LESSON STRUCTURE

The most successful order of presentation for the lessons is outlined below:
- Greeting the students in English
- Oral questions (20 to 30 minutes)

Oral Questions may be done before or after the new lesson has been introduced.
The order suggested in the Student's Book should be adapted to the needs of the group.
- Introduction of a new lesson or continuation of a past lesson.
- Completion of exercises and / or partner activities
- Ending with a more relaxed conversational activity

VOCABULARY

The new words introduced in each lesson are listed under the title and may be introduced in any of the following ways:
- The teacher may write the words on the blackboard and use them in sentences.
- The teacher can dramatize, draw or use the pictures to explain the words.
- The students can work in small groups with their dictionaries.

ORAL QUESTIONS

The oral questions are designed to provide practice in speaking.
The questions and answers stress grammatical structure, and word order of the English language.
When our students completed surveys where Oral Questions were rated "helpful / not helpful" on a scale of 1 to 10, **Oral Questions were consistently rated as "10 - very helpful".**
Teaching this Conversational English program without using the oral questions will result in the lessons becoming too difficult for the students.

These questions provide the basic models of the English Language.
They are a vital part of the program, giving practice, review and an opportunity for the teacher to expand the language to talk about local events.

TESTS

The tests are a part of the learning process. They allow the students to identify the areas they need to study. When marking the sentence answers, subtract one mark for each error.
- If a student has one mistake, he or she will get 3 marks for that answer
- If a student has two mistakes, he or she will get 2 marks for that answer
- If a student has three mistakes, he or she will get 1 mark for that answer
- If a student has four or more mistakes, he or she won't get any marks

GIVE SPECIAL ATTENTION TO INDIVIDUAL NEEDS WHEN MARKING

The teacher should use discretion when marking. Some students work very hard but have difficulty. They should be given the best possible mark. Some students learn easily but become careless, so they should be marked down for their mistakes. In other words, the teacher needs to be aware of the needs of the students. The tests are designed to make most of the students feel good about their English but also give a clear signal to those who aren't making satisfactory progress.

WHAT KIND OF MISTAKES SHOULD BE CONSIDERED?

Marks should be deducted for:
- not knowing the right vocabulary
- word order mistakes
- grammatical errors
- no marks are given if the student doesn't understand the question

Do **not** deduct marks for spelling mistakes if you can understand what the student means.
Students with marks above 80% are ready to continue with the program.
Test answers are included in the Guide.

ANSWERS TO THE ORAL TEST QUESTIONS

The teachers have the choice of having the students answer orally or in writing. As some of the teachers are speaking English as a second language, it might be difficult for them to test pronunciation. If the teacher can understand what the student is saying then the pronunciation should be accepted. Internationally, it is acceptable if the speaker is understood.

The tests are out of 50 except for the last test in Part 1 and in Part 2.
There are no absolutes when assessing test marks. Many factors always enter into the mark. These can range from the student being sick that day to some problem at home. It's also possible that the student missed a lot of classes due to illness.

The purpose of these tests is to allow the students to see where they are having difficulty. This lets them know where they should spend their time when they study.
This is the most important aspect of the tests.

ANSWERS

Answers in the Guide are written in italics. The suggested answers are the most likely, but others are possible.

GLOSSARY

The glossary contains the vocabulary.
The verbs are shown in the infinitive form: do (to.
The past tenses are included for reference in the glossary, shown as: infinitive, past tense.

CONTENTS   LESSONS 21 – 40

This English second language curriculum provided in our Series includes four Modules. Each book has 20 lessons in Part 1 and 20 in Part 2. The new concepts are incrementally introduced. Each lesson is contained in three books for each Part of each book: Student Reader, Student Workbook and Teacher's Guide. The Student Reader can be used a number of times as the students aren't required to write in it.

This Table of Contents includes exercises and activities in the Student Reader, Workbook and Teacher's Guide. It also lists the new concepts, oral activities, written exercises and large and small group activities. Answers are included for all questions and discussions. Unit and final tests are provided.

	Student	Workbook	Guide
Lesson 21	41	47	65

Vocabulary
Short article: Terry Fox
Map
Whole class vocabulary activity
Small group question, answer and check answers activity
Using "even though" and "although"
Using "un" in a word
Using "although" and "even though" in sentences
Match the meaning
Sentence answers to questions
Cloze exercise
Oral questions

	Student	Workbook	Guide
Lesson 22	44	49	68

Vocabulary
Article continued
Small group question, answer and check answers activity
Conditional sentences
Whole class activity using "would, could and should"
Role-play
Tag questions using the conditional
Using "a" and "the"
Word Bingo
Oral questions

Student Reader

	Student	Workbook	Guide
Lesson 23	47	51	70

Article: Rick Hansen
Small group question, answer and check answers activity
Sentence word order
Order of adjectives
Whole class: pictures and questions
Writing sentences using adjectives
Adjective picture exercise
Understanding a joke
Crossword puzzle
Oral questions

	Student	Workbook	Guide
Lesson 24	49	54	73

Vocabulary
Whole class discussion of pictures
Role-play
Written exercise: frequency adverbs
Written exercise: tag questions
Written exercise: cloze exercise
Word Bingo
Oral questions

	Student	Workbook	Guide
Lesson 24 TEST 6			76

	Student	Workbook	Guide
Lesson 25	50	56	78

Vocabulary
Listening and reading orally
Word order for adjectives
Naming body parts
Small group question, answer and check answers activity
Written exercises
Writing sentences to describe pictures
Oral questions

Student Reader

	Student	Workbook	Guide
Lesson 26	52	61	

Vocabulary
Listening and reading orally: Flying in a balloon
Role-play
Small group question, answer and check answers activities
Conditional sentences: untrue fact in the present tense
Conditional sentences: untrue fact in the future tense
Match the meaning
Written exercises
Crossword puzzle
Oral questions

	Student	Workbook	Guide
Lesson 27	55	64	84

Vocabulary
Article: Wright brothers
Small group question, answer and check answers activity
Question and answer picture activity
Match the meaning
Written exercise using "and, even though, although"
Oral questions
Picture enrichment activity

	Student	Workbook	Guide
Lesson 28	57	66	87

Vocabulary
Article: Wright brothers continued
Role-play
Whole class discussion of questions
Small group question, answer and check answers activity
Picture activity
Writing sentence answers
Word order - written
Oral questions

	Student	Workbook	Guide
Lesson 29		TEST 7	89

Student Reader

	Student	Workbook	Guide
Lesson 29	59	68	91

Vocabulary
Article: Gordon Lightfoot – a Canadian artist
Role-play
Using "because"
Using "but"
Small group question, answer and check answers activity
Using "too"
Whole class activity: adding "too" to a sentence.
Match the meaning
Cloze exercise
Writing sentence answers
Oral questions
Competitive team activity

	Student	Workbook	Guide
Lesson 30	61	70	95

Vocabulary
Article: Neil Young – a Canadian musician
Using "get'
Role-play
Writing sentence answers
Completing sentences – using "get"
Match the meaning
Word Bingo
Partner activity – writing sentence answers
Oral questions

	Student	Workbook	Guide
Lesson 31	63	74	98

Vocabulary
Article: The Beatles
Whole class activity using "and, but, because or too"
Small group activity: favorite Beatle songs
Small group question, answer and check answers activity
Cloze exercises
Match the meaning
Writing sentence answers
Oral questions

Student Reader

	Student	Workbook	Guide
Lesson 32	66	76	100

Vocabulary
Article: People Helping People
Small group question, answer and check answers activity
Whole class activity: brainstorming question answers
Article: Earthquake in Haiti
Writing sentence answers
Match the meaning
Partner activity using "if"
Crossword puzzle
Oral questions
Small group activity – arranging cut out words in sentence order

	Student	Workbook	Guide
Lesson 33			104

TEST 8

	Student	Workbook	Guide
Lesson 33	67	79	105

Vocabulary
Role-play: Australia
Legend: Kangaroo
Small group question, answer and check answers activity
Match the meaning
Using descriptive adjectives
Writing sentence answers
Writing a paragraph – guided by questions
Crossword puzzle
Oral questions

	Student	Workbook	Guide
Lesson 34	69	82	

Vocabulary
Role-play: Taj Mahal - India
Small group question, answer and check answers activity
Writing sentence answers
Completing sentences using: "by, about. To, in"
Small group activity: planning a trip
Writing a paragraph about the trip
Crossword puzzle
Oral questions

Student Reader

	Student	Workbook	Guide
Lesson 35	71	85	

Vocabulary
Role-play: Niagara Falls
A joke
Writing sentence answers
Match the meaning
Writing tag questions and answers
Cloze exercise
Word Bingo
Oral questions

	Student	Workbook	Guide
Lesson 36	73	88	

Vocabulary
Role-play: Flying to Whistler in Vancouver, Canada
Small group question, answer and check answers activity
Review: conditional sentences
Using "get"
Completing sentences using "and, but, although, even though, because"
Crossword puzzle
Oral questions review

	Student	Workbook	Guide
Lesson 36 TEST 9			117

	Student	Workbook	Guide
Lesson 37	75	90	118

Vocabulary
Role-play: Shopping at Whistler
Map of Whistler
Reading and following a map
Small group question, answer and check answers activity
Writing sentence answers
Small group activity: Writing sentences that tell locations in Whistler
Small group activity: Shopping at Whistler
Writing a paragraph about the shopping trip
Whole class activity: Recording what others bought at Whistler
Oral questions

Student Reader

		Student	Workbook	Guide
Lesson 38		77	93	119

Vocabulary
Role-play: Skiing at Whistler
Small group question, answer and check answers activity
Whole class oral reading: adding adjectives orally
Small group brainstorming
Cloze exercise: completing paragraph with past tense verbs
Match the Meaning
Whole class activity: sharing and writing interests using role cards
Oral questions

		Student	Workbook	Guide
Lesson 39		79	95	124

Vocabulary
Role-play: The Lost Wallet
Small group question, answer and check answers activity
Match the Meaning
Cloze exercise
Writing sentence answers to questions
Small group activity: Planning a day at Whistler
Completing a social calendar chart for Whistler
Word Bingo
Oral questions review

		Student	Workbook	Guide
Lesson 40	**TEST 10**			129
	Final Test for Book 2			

Printing Instructions for this Document

Student Reader   Pages 13 – 45
Student Workbook   Pages 48 – 95
Teacher's Guide   Pages 98 – 163

Student Reader

Beginners ESL Lesson Plans Book 2

Student Reader

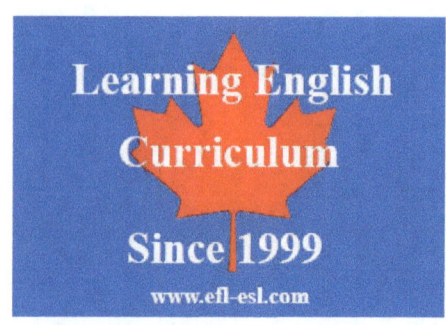

Student Reader

Lesson 21

VOCABULARY:	across from	on the right	movie	opposite
along	turn (to)	lunch	on the left	belong (to)
corner	get (to)	block	when	store

ACTVITY 1: Listen to your teacher read the paragraphs and watch the video. Then take turns reading the sentences orally.

The Carters live on Kent Street at number 11. Raymond and Ruth walk along Wilson Street to their school. They walk two blocks to school.

To go to the supermarket, they walk along Kent Street to West Street, they turn right and walk two blocks. The supermarket is on the right.

The Carters and their friends like to go to the theater to see a movie. The theater is at the corner of Main Street and Wilson Street.

Mr. Carter has lunch in the restaurant across from the park.

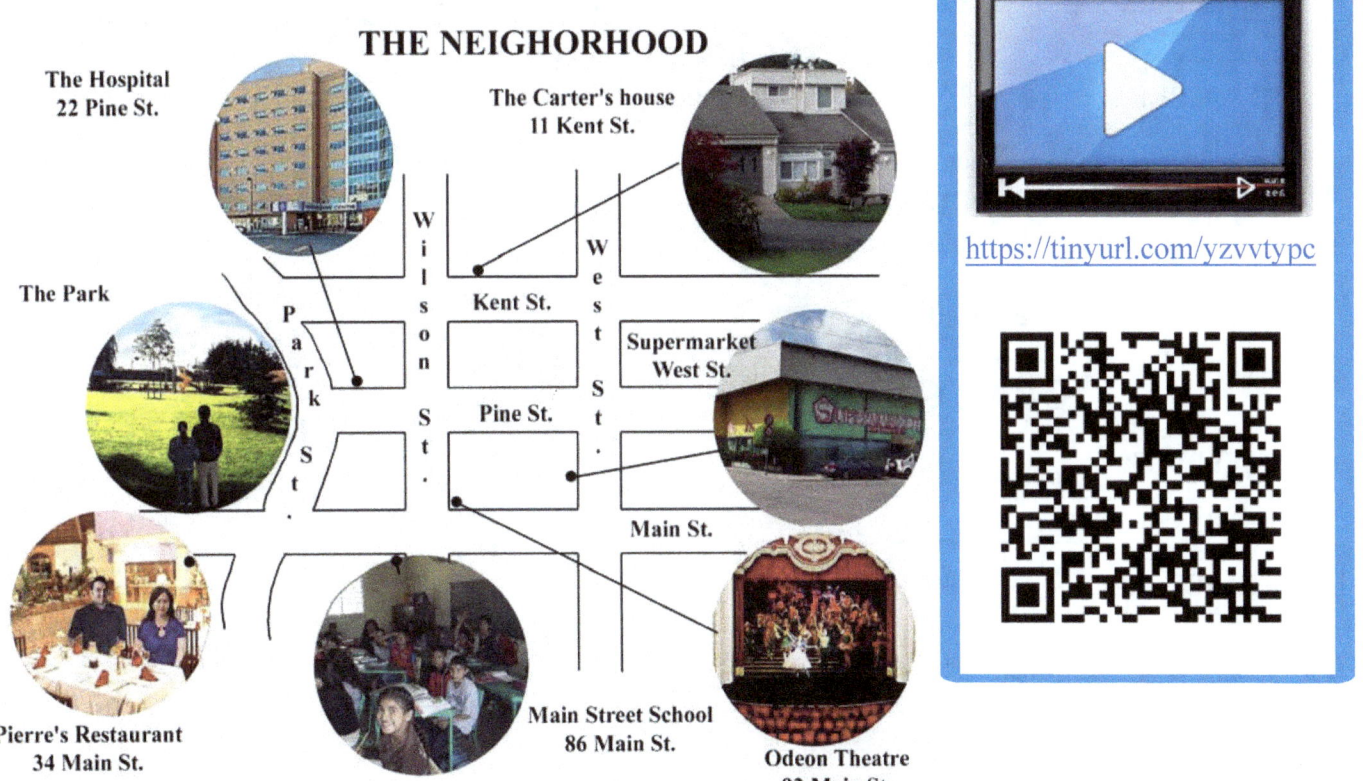

https://tinyurl.com/yzvvtypc

Student Reader

Lesson 21 Continued

Look at the map on Page 38. Listen to the video first. Divide into small groups and ask each other these questions. Then look at the answers. If you use a number, use "at". If you don't use a number, use "on".

1. Where is the hospital?
2. Where is the Odeon Theater?
3. What is the address of the school?
4. Where is the supermarket?
5. Where is Pierre's Restaurant?
6. What is the Carter's address?

1. The hospital is on Pine Street. The church is at 22 Pine Street.
2. The Odeon Theater is on Main Street. The Odeon Theater is at 93 Main Street.
3. The school's address is: 86 Main Street.
4. The supermarket is on West Street.
5. Pierre's Restaurant is at 34 Main Street. Pierre's Restaurant is on Main Street.
6. The Carter's address is: 11 Kent Street.

Exercise 1 – Workbook Page 43

THE USE OF "ANY"

EXAMPLES:

To ask a question when the answer is <u>singular</u>:

Do you have a hamburger?   Yes, I have a hamburger.   No, I don't have a hamburger.

To ask a question when the answer is <u>plural</u>:

How many hamburgers do you have?   I have six hamburgers.
I don't have any hamburgers.

Do you have some hamburgers?   I have some hamburgers.
I don't have any hamburgers.

ORAL QUESTIONS

ACTIVITY 3   WORKBOOK PAGE 43
EXERCISE 2   WORKBOOK PAGE 44
EXERCISE 3   WORKBOOK PAGE 44

TEACHER'S GUIDE

ACTIVITY 4 – WORKBOOK PAGE 45

BINGO

DIRECTIONS: First the students are to match the meaning by writing the number of the meanings in List 2 beside the words in List 1.
EXAMPLE: 1 corner

Next, they are to write the words in List 1 into the BINGO squares.
Then the meanings in List 2 can be called to begin playing the game.
For instructions on how to play see Page 73 of Book 1 Part 1 of Guide.
Bingo Answers Guide Page 86

Student Reader

Lesson 22

VOCABULARY:

supper	machine	guide	about
each	time	volunteer (to)	tourist	trail
after	other	both	mountain	sew (to)
	enjoy (to)	on the way		often hike (to)

https://tinyurl.com/5n6sazrv

ACTIVITY 1: Listen to your teacher and repeat each name.

DAYS OF THE WEEK:

Sunday   Monday   Tuesday   Wednesday
Thursday   Friday   Saturday

ACTIVITY 2: Listen to your teacher read the paragraphs, then take turns reading the sentences orally.

Interesting Activities!

The Carters enjoy many things. Raymond's parents like to go to the church/temple/synogue. They sometimes go on Sundays.

Ruth likes to sew. She also works as a volunteer at the hospital. Her friend Nancy likes to sew, too. They both volunteer on Saturdays and Sundays and go to the movies on Saturday night. They usually buy something to eat on the way home.

Raymond and his friend Ming go hiking along the mountain trails. They usually hike after school on Mondays and Wednesdays. Sometimes they volunteer as guides for tourists who have come to town. They often buy some hamburgers on the way home.

ACTIVITY 3: Video corresponds to passage above and questions in workbook

Divide into small groups and ask each other these questions.

1. Do you like to hike along mountain trails?
2. Do you ever volunteer?
3. Do you like to go to the movies?
4. Do you like to talk to tourists?
5. What do you have for supper?

1. Yes, I like to hike along mountain trails.
   No, I don't like to hike along mountain trails.
2. Yes, I volunteer.
   No, I don't volunteer.
3. Yes, I like to go to the movies.
   No, I don't like to go to the movies.
4. Yes, I like to talk to tourists.
   No, I don't like to talk to tourists.
5. I have _____ for supper.

They buy some hamburgers **on the way home.**

   They have supper **at home.**   After the basketball game they **go home.**

Lesson 22 Continued

EXERCISES 1 AND 2 – WORKBOOK PAGE 46

ACTIVITY 4:   ASK YOUR PARTNER.   ANSWER IN SENTENCES.

1. What do you like to do?
2. What days do you go to school?
3. Where do you usually eat supper?
4. Do you like to hike?
5. Do you like hamburgers?
6. Do you like sewing?
7. What days do you do interesting things?
8. Do you eat something on the way home from school?
9. Do you ever do volunteer work?
10. What do you like to eat?

https://tinyurl.com/nehj3xpd

EXERCISES 3 AND 4 – WORKBOOK PAGE 47

ACTIVITY 5:   ORAL QUESTIONS   TEACHER'S GUIDE

Each student is to choose one picture from below. They are to ask a partner these questions.

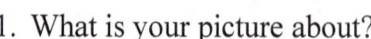
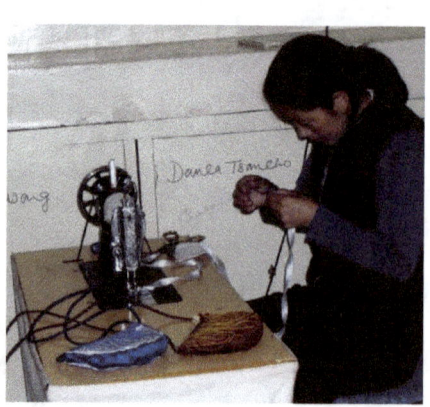

1. What is your picture about?
2. Do you go there?
3. When do you go there?
4. What do you do there?
5. Does your friend go there too?

Student Reader

Lesson 23

VOCABULARY:

through	decide (to)	see (to)	snow	sure [yes]
top	deep	clothes	head (to)	try (to)
warm	cannot [can't]	whose	near	small

ACTIVITY 1: Read the dialogue with your teacher and watch the video.
Divide into groups of two or three and role-play.

https://tinyurl.com/mrezaf6r

Narrator: Sarah and Peter are hiking on a mountain near their home.
Sarah: I can see the top.
Peter: But we can't see the other side.
Sarah: The snow is deep here.
Peter: It's deeper at the top of the mountain!
Sarah: Can you walk through deep snow, Peter?
Peter: Sure. Can you?
Sarah: I want to try.
Peter: Do you want to go to the top of the mountain?
Sarah: Sure. We can't see the mountains on the other side from up there.
Peter: Let's try to get to the top.
Sarah: Okay. We have warm clothes.
Narrator: Peter and Sarah head up the snowy mountain.

ACTIVITY 2: Divide into groups. Ask and answer the questions, then look at the answers.

1. Where are Sarah and Peter?
2. Are they standing in some snow?
3. Where is the snow deeper?
4. Do they have warm clothes?
5. Where do they want to go?
6. Do they head up to the top of the mountain?

1. They are on a mountain near their home.
2. Yes, they are standing in some snow.
3. It's deeper at the top of the mountain.
4. Yes, they have warm clothes.
5. They want to go to the top of the mountain.
6. Yes, they head up the mountain.

EXERCISES 1, 2 & 3 – WORKBOOK PAGE 48 & 49
ACTIVITY 3 WORKBOOK PAGE 50 ACTIVITY 4
TEACHER'S GUIDE PAGE 91 & 92

ORAL QUESTIONS TEACHER'S GUIDE

Student Reader

Lesson 24

VOCABULARY:
up	beautiful	idea	below	extend (to)
stretch (to)	food	place	dictionary	

ACTIVITY 1: Role-play the dialogue with your teacher. Then role-play it in small groups.

https://tinyurl.com/yckzfc9f

Narrator: Sarah and Peter hike up the mountain.
Peter: It's beautiful.
Sarah: I can see the town below us. It looks small from here.
Peter: Can you see the building where we live?
Sarah: It's the big building on the right.
Peter: It looks like it. I'm sure it is.

Narrator: They hike up the mountain.
Sarah: The snow is deep!
Peter: We're near the top.
Sarah: Here we are! Look at those snowy mountains!
Peter: Wow! They stretch on and on.
Sarah: Now we can enjoy them and have something to eat.
Peter: Good idea!

ACTIVITY 2:

Divide into small groups. Ask and answer the questions. Then look at the answers.

1. What are Sarah and Peter hiking through?
2. What is it like up there?
3. How does the town look?
4. What can they see below them?
5. Where is their building?
6. Is the snow deeper near the top of the mountain?

1. They are hiking through the snow.
2. It's beautiful.
3. The town looks small.
4. They can see the town. They can see their building.
5. It's on the right.
6. Yes, it's deeper near the top.

EXERCISE 1 & 2- WORKBOOK PAGE 51 ACTIVITY 3 & EXERCISE 3 - WORKBOOK PAGE 52
EXERCISE 4 – WORKBOOK PAGE 53

TEST 6 TEACHER'S GUIDE PAGES 94-95

Student Reader

Lesson 25

THE PAST TENSE

VOCABULARY: basketball
close (to)   morning   last night   last week
night   watch (to) letter   last weekend
yesterday   year   play (to)   regular
make (to)   phone (to) follow (to) afternoon

https://tinyurl.com/3pu3ub7b

PRESENT TENSE

Ruth <u>plays</u> basketball today.

PAST TENSE

Ruth <u>played</u> basketball yesterday.

The regular past tense = play + ed

Ruth *played* basketball yesterday.

Many questions use "to do" in the past tense. It isn't regular.

Present Tense
I do
you do
he, she, it does
we do
you do
they do

Past Tense
I did
you did
he, she, it did
we did
you did
they did

When <u>did</u> Ruth play basketball?
Ruth played basketball last week.

<u>Did</u> Ruth play basketball last week?
Yes, Ruth played basketball last week.

Student Reader

Lesson 25 Continued

REFERENCES FOR PRONUNCIATION OF - ED AT THE END OF A WORD.
Many past tense regular verbs end in - ed.   - ed has three different sounds.

REGULAR VERBS

The -ed sounds as in do	The -ed sounds as in toy.	The -ed sounds as in Edward.
to play – played		
to live - lived	to watch – watched	to need - needed
to enjoy - enjoyed	to walk – walked	to want - wanted
to follow – followed	to like – liked	
to phone – phoned	to ask - asked	
to close - closed	to practice - practiced	
to answer – answered		

ACTIVITY 1: Listen to the "ed" endings and repeat the words after your teacher.

1. The -ed sounds as in do
Examples: followed   played   lived   answered

2. The -ed sounds as in toy.
Words that end in: p, ss, k, ce, ch, sh, *plus* - ed are usually pronounced with the t sound.
Examples: watched,   walked   liked   asked   hiked

3. The -ed sounds as in Edward.
Examples: needed   wanted

ACTIVITY 2:

Listen to your teacher read each paragraph and watch the video. Then take turns reading the sentences orally and identify the regular past tense verb(s) in the sentence

It snowed in the night. It was warmer in the morning and the snow became water. All the streets were wet, and there was some rain. The people who went to town carried umbrellas.

Last year Raymond and his friend Ming hiked up the mountain trail. They belonged to a hiking group. All the boys and girls in the group enjoyed the snowy mountains. It usually snowed at night. The trees looked beautiful under the snow.

EXERCISES 1, 2 AND 3 – WORKBOOK PAGE 54
ACTIVITY 5 – TEACHER'S GUIDE PAGE 97

ORAL QUESTIONS   TEACHER'S GUIDE

Student Reader

Lesson 25 Continued

ACTIVITY 3 Divide into small groups. Ask and answer each question in a sentence.

Then check your answer.
To do is not a regular verb. The past tense of to do is did.

Did you play basketball yesterday?
Yes, I played basketball yesterday.

No, I did not play basketball yesterday.
No, I didn't play basketball yesterday.

Yes = past tense (played)
No = past tense = did + not + play = contraction = didn't play

https://tinyurl.com/mrzs8smf

1. Did you phone your friend last night?	1. Yes, I phoned my friend last night. No, I didn't phone my friend last night.
2. Did you watch television last night?	2. Yes, I watched television last night. No, I didn't watch television last night.
3. Did you live here last year?	3. Yes, I lived here last year. No, I didn't live here last year.
4. Did you enjoy the theater last week?	4. Yes, I enjoyed the theater last week. No, I didn't enjoy the theater last week.
5. Did you eat in a restaurant last night? (ate)	5. Yes, I ate in a restaurant last night. No, I didn't eat in a restaurant last night.
6. Did the teacher close the door?	6. Yes, the teacher closed the door. No, the teacher didn't close the door.
7. Did your dog follow you today?	7. Yes, my dog followed me today. No, my dog didn't follow me today.
8. Did you live in the United States last year?	8. Yes, I lived in the United States last year. No, I didn't live in the United States last year.
9. Did you talk to your friend yesterday afternoon?	9. Yes, I talked to my friend yesterday afternoon? No, I didn't talk to my friend yesterday afternoon.
10. Did you answer the telephone last night?	10. Yes, I answered the telephone last night. No, I didn't answer the telephone last night.

EXERCISES 4 AND 5 – **WORKBOOK PAGE 55**

ACTIVITY 4:

Look at the pictures and answer orally in sentences, using a regular past tense verb.

What did they do?

Student Reader

Lesson 26

VOCABULARY:

store	library	sometimes	later	something
put (to)	begin (to)	meet (to)	soccer	road
song	ticket	music	infinitive	listen (to)

IRREGULAR VERBS IN THE PAST TENSE

EXAMPLES

TO GO	TO HAVE	TO SEE
I went	I had	I saw
you went	you had	you saw
he/she/it went	he/she/it had	he/she/it saw
we went	we had	we saw
you went	you had	you saw
they went	they had	they saw

to find - *found*	begin - *began* to	to come - *came*
to write - *wrote*	eat - *ate*	to buy - *bought*
to put - *put*	to read - *read* to	to meet - *met*
to sit - *sat*	study - *studied*	

ACTIVITY 1:

Listen to your teacher read this paragraph and then take turns reading the sentences orally.

ON SATURDAYS

The Carters went to town on Saturdays last month. Craig Carter usually went to the video store and Jessica found books in the library. Sometimes Ruth saw good CD's in the music store. Raymond usually met his friends outside the theater. Later in the afternoon, they sometimes bought pizza for supper.

WORKBOOK – EXERCISE 1 PAGE 56

* When a question has "did", answer in the past tense!

NEGATIVE ANSWERS

If the answer is **yes**, you use the past tense of the main verb.
Did you *have* a pen? Yes, I <u>had</u> a pen.
If the answer is **no**, use the past tense of "**to do**" + the **main verb**.
Did you *have* a pen? No, I <u>didn't have</u> a pen.

I <u>played</u> basketball last night. Did you play basketball, too?

No, I <u>didn't play</u> basketball, I played soccer.

Student Reader

Lesson 26 Continued

ACTIVITY 2:

Divide into groups of two or three. Ask and answer each question.
Then read the answer in the box.

https://tinyurl.com/mr22ey8v

1. Did you buy a book yesterday?
2. Did you go to town last week?
3. Did you have some hamburgers for lunch?
4. Did you study your English last night?
5. Did you find your friend yesterday?
6. Did you write in your notebook?
7. Did you sit in a restaurant last night?
8. Did you come to English class?
9. Did you meet your friend this morning?
10. Did you see your mother last night?

1. Yes, I bought a book yesterday.
   No, I didn't buy a book yesterday.
2. Yes, I went to town last week.
   No, I didn't go to town last week.
3. Yes, I had some hamburgers for lunch.
   No, I didn't have any hamburgers for lunch.
4. Yes, I studied my English last night.
   No, I didn't study my English last night.
5. Yes, I found my friend yesterday.
   No, I didn't find my friend yesterday.
6. Yes, I wrote in my notebook this morning.
   No, I didn't write in my notebook this morning.
7. Yes, I sat in a restaurant last night.
   No, I didn't sit in a restaurant last night.
8. Yes, I came to English class yesterday.
   No, I didn't come to English class yesterday.
9. Yes, I met my friend this morning.
   No, I didn't meet my friend this morning.
10. Yes, I saw my mother last night.
    No, I didn't see my mother last night.

WORKBOOK – EXERCISE 2 PAGE 56
WORKBOOK – ACTIVITY 3 PAGE 56
WORKBOOK – EXERCISES 3 AND 4 PAGE 57
WORKBOOK - ACTIVITY 4 PAGE 58
BINGO ANSWERS GUIDE PAGE 101

ORAL QUESTIONS

TEACHER'S GUIDE

Student Reader

LESSON 27

VOCABULARY: inside   was not [wasn't]   were not [weren't]
cook (to)   weekend

Sometimes a past tense question uses the verb "to be".

PRESENT TENSE	PAST TENSE
I am	I was
you are	you were
he / she / it is	he / she / it was
we are	we were
you are	you were
they are	they were

EXAMPLES: Where **were** you?   **Weren't** you here yesterday?
NOTE: I **was** at the theater.   No, I **wasn't** here yesterday.

The second person singular <u>always</u> uses the plural form –
you <u>are</u>, you <u>were</u>.

Listen to your teacher read the dialogue. Then role-play it with a partner.

https://tinyurl.com/5af2mrzw

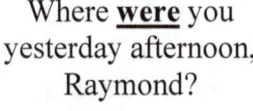
Where **were** you yesterday afternoon, Raymond?

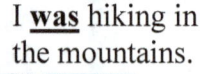
I **was** hiking in the mountains.

Wasn't Ruth hiking with you?

No, she **wasn't**. She **was** at the hospital.

ACTIVITY 1   WHOLE CLASS ACTIVITY
ANSWER ORALLY IN SENTENCES

1. Were you at home last night?
2. Were you at the theater last week?
3. Was your dog outside last night?
4. Was your door closed last night?
5. Was your friend at a restaurant?
6. Was your friend in class yesterday?
7. Were you in town yesterday?
8. Were your friends at a restaurant last Saturday?
9. Were you in the library this morning?
10. Were you at the movies last week?

EXERCISES 1 AND 2 WORKBOOK PAGES 59 AND 60
ACTIVITY 2 WORKBOOK PAGE 59   ACTIVITY 2 GUIDE PAGES 103 and 104

ORAL QUESTIONS   TEACHER'S GUIDE

Student Reader

LESSON 28 REVIEW

ORAL QUESTIONS — TEACHER'S GUIDE

ACTIVITY 1: WHOLE CLASS ACTIVITY — ANSWER ORALLY IN SENTENCES

Ask each other these questions.

1. Are you in this picture?
2. Do you think they are students?
3. Is it cold outside?
4. What do you think they are talking about?
5. Are they eating?
6. Are they in a restaurant?

EXERCISE 1 – WORKBOOK PAGE 61

EXERCISE 2 – WORKBOOK PAGE 61

Student Reader

Lesson 28 Continued

ACTIVITY 2:

Divide into small groups. Ask and answer each question, then look at the answers in the box.

1. Were you studying English last night?
2. Was your friend at your home yesterday?
3. Does your friend live across the road from you?
4. Were you at the theater last week?
5. Did you walk along the road this morning?
6. Were you cooking chicken yesterday?
7. Were you watching a video last night?
8. Did you do volunteer work last month?

https://tinyurl.com/k4jfc47y

1. Yes, I was studying English last night.
   No, I wasn't studying English last night.
2. Yes, my friend was at my home yesterday.
   No, my friend wasn't at my home yesterday.
3. Yes, my friend lives across the road from me.
   No, my friend doesn't live across the road from me.
4. Yes, I was at the theater last week.
   No, I wasn't at the theater last week.
5. Yes, I walked along the road this morning.
   No, I didn't walk along the road this morning.
6. Yes, I was cooking chicken yesterday.
   No, I wasn't cooking chicken yesterday.
7. Yes, I was watching a video last night.
   No, I wasn't watching a video last night.
8. Yes, I did volunteer work last month.
   No, I didn't do volunteer work last month.

ACTIVITY 3 – GUIDE PAGES 105   TEST 7 GUIDE PAGES 106-107

Student Reader

Lesson 29

WHEN IN THE PAST?

VOCABULARY:

post (to)	then	breakfast	attend (to)
arrive (to)	before	minute	hour
evening	weekend	ago	TV = television

Listen to your teacher read the sentences. Then take turns reading them orally.

*
I was at home **yesterday**.	I saw my friend **the day before yesterday**.
I arrived **ten minutes ago**.	I phoned my friend **an hour ago**.
I went to Delhi **last year**.	I went to town **last weekend**.

ORAL QUESTIONS   TEACHER'S GUIDE

WORD ORDER

Put <u>when something happens</u> at the end of a sentence.

EXAMPLE	I	went	to	town	yesterday.
	(subject)	(verb)	(preposition)	(object)	(when)

[ACTIVITY 2 – WORKBOOK PAGE 62](#)

[EXERCISE 1 – WORKBOOK PAGE 62](#)

[EXERCISE 2 – WORKBOOK PAGE 63](#)

[ACTIVITY 3 - WORKBOOK PAGES 63 and 64](#)

Student Reader

Lesson 29 Continued

ACTIVITY 1 Watch the video then divide into small groups. Ask and answer these questions.

https://tinyurl.com/yc5973ej

Did you go to town the day before yesterday?

Were you at home yesterday afternoon?

Did you get to class ten minutes ago?

Did you eat breakfast before you came to class?

Did you meet your friend an hour ago?

Did you make some hamburgers the day before yesterday?

Was it cold outside this morning?

Did you play basketball last weekend?

Were you living in New York a year ago?

Did you have some tea an hour ago?

1. Yes, I went to town the day before yesterday. No, I didn't go to town the day before yesterday.
2. Yes, I was at home yesterday afternoon. No, I wasn't at home yesterday afternoon.
3. Yes, I got to class ten minutes ago. No, I didn't get to class ten minutes ago.
4. Yes, I ate breakfast before I came to class. No, I didn't eat breakfast before I came to class.
5. Yes, I met my friend an hour ago. No, I didn't meet my friend an hour ago.
6. Yes, I made some hamburgers the day before yesterday? No, I didn't make any hamburgers the day before yesterday.
7. Yes, it was cold outside this morning. No, it wasn't cold outside this morning.
8. Yes, I played basketball last weekend. No, I didn't play basketball last weekend.
9. Yes, I was living in New York a year ago. No, I wasn't living in New York a year ago.
10. Yes, I had some tea an hour ago. No, I didn't have any tea an hour ago.

ACTIVITY 4   GUIDE PAGE 110

Student Reader

Lesson 30

VOCABULARY:	specific	progressive tense	happen (to)	hungry
pair of shoes	ready	use (to)	fish	cry (to)
pair of gloves	wear (to)	rain (to)	another	every
Chinese food	cook (to)	plane (airplane)	fry (to)	feet

https://tinyurl.com/yshvec6f

THE PRESENT PROGRESSIVE

The progressive tenses are sometimes called the continuous tenses.
The progressive tenses show that something is happening at a specific time.

For the present progressive use the present tense of the verb
"to be" (am / is / are) + the present participle.

For the present participle, add "ing" to the root of the infinitive.

EXAMPLES: to play - **playing**   I **am reading** a book.
                                        She **is drinking** juice.
to see - **seeing**   to be - **being**   We **are learning** English.

When you add an ending to a word that ends with <u>one silent</u> "e",
drop the "e", then add the ending.

EXAMPLES: to have – **having**   to close – **closing**   to live – **living**

ORAL QUESTIONS   TEACHER'S GUIDE

WORKBOOK EXERCISES 1, 2, AND 3 PAGE 65

ACTIVITY 2   Divide into groups of three and listen to your teacher read the dialogue.
Then role-play it two or three times.

Narrator: Peter arrives at Sarah's house. She is in another room.

Peter: What are you doing, Sarah?

Sarah: I'm trying on my new blue dress.

Peter: Okay, but I'm hungry.

Sarah: Are we eating at 7:00?

Peter: Yes, and it's 6:45 now.

Narrator: Sarah comes into the room.

Peter: Wow! You're looking great.

Sarah: Thanks, Peter. Are we having Chinese food?

Peter: Sure. Our friends are cooking it now. Can we go?

Sarah: I'm ready and I'm hungry, too.

https://tinyurl.com/2ms2nx6k

WORKBOOK – EXERCISES 4 AND 5, + ACTIVITY 1 PAGE 66

Student Reader

Lesson 31

VOCABULARY:

stop (to)	these	dinner	laugh (to)	paint (to)
sleep (to)	radio	day-off	work (to)	ride (to)
foot (singular)	feet (plural)	syllable	computer	while
swim (to)	wear (to)	feel (to)	consonant	vowel

SPELLING

One vowel and two consonants:

sit + t + ing = sitting   stop + p + ed = stopped

EXERCISE 1 — WORKBOOK PAGE 67

Two vowels and one consonant:

meet + ing = meeting   look + ed = looked
see + ing = seeing   need + ed = needed

EXERCISE 2 — WORKBOOK PAGE 67
EXERCISE 3 — WORKBOOK PAGE 67
EXERCISE 4 — WORKBOOK PAGE 67

When the verb ends in a silent single "e", drop the "e" before adding "ing" (live - living)

EXERCISE 5 — WORKBOOK PAGE 67

ORAL QUESTIONS TEACHER'S GUIDE

EXERCISES 6 AND 7 — WORKBOOK PAGE 68
ACTIVITY 3 — WORKBOOK PAGE 69

SPELLING FOR SOME VERBS WITH "ED" AND "ING".
(The irregular forms are underlined.)

answer	answering	answered	arrive	arriving	arrived
be	being	was/were	come	coming	came
close	closing	closed	cook	cooking	cooked
drink	drinking	drank	drive	driving	drove
eat	eating	ate	have	having	had
meet	meeting	met	phone	phoning	phoned
put	putting	put	rain	raining	rained
sit	sitting	sat	stop	stopping	stopped
swim	swimming	swam	wear	wearing	wore

Student Reader

Lesson 31 Continued

ACTIVITY 1:

First watch the video - answer the questions in unison. Next, Divide into small groups. Ask and answer these questions, then look at the answers in the box.

1. Is it raining outside?
2. Did it snow yesterday?
3. Were you at home last night?
4. Did you have a day-off from school last week?
5. Did you stop beside the road this morning?
6. Were you sleeping last night?
7. Were you eating chicken for dinner last night?
8. Did you learn to swim last year?

https://tinyurl.com/3xhtnmyd

Yes, it's raining outside.
No, it isn't raining outside.

Yes, it snowed yesterday.
No, it didn't snow yesterday.

Yes, I was at home last night.
No, I wasn't at home last night.

Yes, I had a day-off from school last week.
No, I didn't have a day-off from school last week.

Yes, I stopped beside the road this morning.
No, I didn't stop beside the road this morning.

Yes, I was sleeping last night.
No, I wasn't sleeping last night.

Yes, I was eating chicken for dinner last night.
No, I wasn't eating chicken for dinner last night.

Yes, I learned to swim last year.
No, I didn't learn to swim last year.

ACTIVITY 2 FIND A PARTNER; ANSWER ORALLY IN SENTENCES

You can answer all the questions?

How do you feel?

Student Reader

Lesson 32 — REVIEW

VOCABULARY: umbrella   archery   fly (to)

Listen to your teacher read the sentences under the pictures and the paragraph. Then take turns reading the sentences orally.

THE PRESENT PROGRESSIVE TENSE REVIEW

She is playing basketball.

He is practicing archery.

THE CARTER'S FRIDAY NIGHTS

On Friday night, no one but Toto is at home in the Carter's house.
Ruth plays basketball. She is playing on her school team.
Raymond is practicing archery.
He practices three times a week on Mondays, Wednesdays and Fridays.
Jessica and Craig are watching a movie at the theater.
Their dog, Toto, is at home. He is sleeping.

ACTIVITY 1 Divide into small groups. Ask each other:

What do you do on Friday nights?

Answer in sentences.

https://tinyurl.com/mryypc5p

What is going up when the rain is coming down?

EXERCISES 1, 2 AND 3   WORKBOOK PAGES 70 and 71
ACTIVITY 2   GUIDE PAGE 115   TEST 8 GUIDE PAGES 116-117

Student Reader

Lesson 33

VOCABULARY:

traditional	music	afternoon	blue jeans (jeans)	through
donkey	party	park		

The progressive tenses show that something is happening at a <u>specific time</u>.
For the past progressive tense use the past tense of the verb
"to be" (was / were) <u>+ the present participle.</u>

EXAMPLES:

I was walking yesterday. We were walking yesterday.
You were walking yesterday. You were walking yesterday.
He was walking yesterday. They were walking yesterday.
She was walking yesterday.
It was walking yesterday.

EXAMPLE:

Ruth **was playing** basketball yesterday morning.

ACTIVITY 1

Divide into small groups, look at each picture and answer the question in sentences.

1. What are they doing?

2. Where are they going?

3. What are they watching?

ORAL QUESTIONS   TEACHER'S GUIDE

| EXERCISES 1 AND 2 | WORKBOOK PAGES 72 | EXERCISE 3 | WORKBOOK PAGE 73 |

Student Reader

Lesson 33 Continued

ACTIVITY 2 First listen to the audio and answer (Yes and No) in unison.
Then Divide into groups of two or three. Ask each other these questions.

1. Were you eating fish last night?
2. Were you drinking apple juice this morning?
3. Were you eating a hamburger last night?
4. Are you living across from a church? .
5. Are you studying English?
6. Are you living beside your friend?
7. Were you phoning your friend last night?
8. Were you enjoying the theater last week?
9. Were you putting your umbrella up today?
10. Were you wearing blue jeans the day before yesterday?
11. Was the rain coming down this morning?
12. Were you listening to music while you studied?

https://tinyurl.com/3d6bm34p

1. Yes, I was eating fish last night.
   No, I wasn't eating fish last night.
2. Yes, I was drinking apple juice this morning.
   No, I wasn't drinking apple juice this morning.
3. Yes, I was eating a hamburger last night.
   No, I wasn't eating a hamburger last night.
4. Yes, I'm living across from a church.
   No, I'm not living across from a church.
5. Yes, I'm studying English.
   No, I'm not studying English.
6. Yes, I'm living beside my friend.
   No, I'm not living beside my friend.
7. Yes, I was phoning my friend last night.
   No, I wasn't phoning my friend last night.
8. Yes, I was enjoying the theater last week.
   No, I wasn't enjoying the theater last week.
9. Yes, I was putting my umbrella up today.
   No, I wasn't putting my umbrella up today.
10. Yes, I was wearing blue jeans the day before yesterday.
    No, I wasn't wearing blue jeans the day before yesterday.
11. Yes, the rain was coming down this morning.
    No, the rain wasn't coming down this morning.
12. Yes, I was listening to music while I studied.
    No, I wasn't listening to music while I studied.

ACTIVITY 3 GUIDE PAGES 120, 121, WORKBOOK PAGE 73

Student Reader

Lesson 34

VOCABULARY:	phrase		
talk (to)	short	lake	anyone
nearby	return (to)	late	bed
noon	thing	midnight	anything

MONTHS OF THE YEAR:			
January	February	March	April
May	June	July	August
September	October	November	December

NOTE: The western calendar begins the week with Sunday. A weekend is Saturday and Sunday.

NOTE: We use "at" when referring to a short time or <u>a specific time</u>.
"at night" is an exception.

Put <u>when something happens</u> at the end of the sentence.

*
in the morning	in the afternoon	in the evening
at noon	at night	at midnight
at breakfast	at lunch	at supper (at dinner)

ACTIVITY 1 Divide into small groups. Ask each other these questions and then look at the answers. Use the phrases above to answer the questions in sentences.

1. When do you eat breakfast?
2. When do you eat lunch?
3. When do you go to bed?
4. When are you sleeping?
5. When are you walking outside?

TEACHER'S GUIDE
1. I eat breakfast at _____ .
   I eat breakfast in the morning.
2. I eat lunch at _____ .
3. I go to bed _____ .
4. I'm sleeping _____ .
5. I'm walking outside _____ .

EXERCISES 1, 2 AND 3 [WORKBOOK PAGE 74](#)

ORAL QUESTIONS

ACTIVITY 2	[WORKBOOK PAGE 75](#)
EXERCISE 4	[WORKBOOK PAGE 75](#)
ACTIVITY 3	[GUIDE PAGE 123](#)
ACTIVITY 4	[GUIDE PAGES 124 - 127](#)

Student Reader

LESSON 35

VOCABULARY:

holiday	marry (to)	tomorrow	next
visit (to)	for	couple	let (to)
stay (to)	idea	will	let us [let's]
reservation	which	will not [won't]	bus

THE SIMPLE FUTURE TENSE
When someone is talking about something that will happen in the future, the future tense is used.

I **will drive** to town tomorrow.
Use: will + the root form of the verb = will drive
Negative: I will not drive. = I won't drive.

Examples of the future tense:

To drive:

Singular:

I will drive.   *I'll drive.*
You will drive.   *You'll drive.*
He will drive.   *He'll drive.*
She will drive.   *She'll drive.*
It will drive.   *It'll drive.*

Plural:

We will drive.   *We'll drive.*
You will drive.   *You'll drive.*
They will drive. *They'll drive.*

To be

I will be	we will be	I will not (won't) be…	we will not (won't) be…
you will be	you will be	you will not (won't) be…	you will not (won't) be…
he will be	they will be	he will not (won't) be…	they will not (won't) be…
she will be		she will not (won't) be…	
it will be		it will not (won't) be…	

ACTIVITY 1:   Read these sentences orally, and change them to the future tense.

It is cold in the mountains.   They hike through the snow.
There are many birds in the trees.   They see their friends on Saturday night.

NOTE: In Britain, "**shall**" is sometimes used to express future time but it is seldom used in Canada or in The United States.

Where shall we go?   We shall go to town.

Student Reader

Lesson 35 Continued

ORAL QUESTIONS   TEACHER'S GUIDE

EXERCISES 1 AND 2 WORKBOOK PAGE 76

EXERCISE 3 WORKBOOK PAGE 77

ACTIVITY 2:   Divide into groups of four or five. Role-play and then change roles.

Narrator: Luke and Rose are a married couple. They are living in India.
They want to go for a holiday.
They are asking Carol and Tom, who are visiting India, to go with them.

Rose: I want to have a holiday. What about going to Delhi?
Luke: That's a great idea! Let's ask Tom and Carol to come with us.
Rose: We'll ask them tomorrow.

Narrator: The next morning Luke and Rose meet Tom and Carol at school.

Rose: Hi, We're glad to see you.
Luke: We want to go to Delhi for a holiday.
Rose: We don't have any classes next week. Will you come with us?

Carol: Do we have the time, Tom?
Tom: Sure, let's go.

Rose: Let's go next weekend. Will that be okay?
Tom: It's good for us.

Carol: Where will we stay?
Rose: Let's stay at the Peace Hotel.
Luke: Good idea! They speak English.

Carol: Will you phone for a hotel reservation, Rose?
Rose: Sure.

Luke: When will we go?
Tom: Let's go on the night bus next Friday. We'll get to Delhi in the morning.
Carol: Great, the bus stops beside the Peace Hotel.

Luke: We'll see you on the bus on Friday.

https://tinyurl.com/3vs8z4hm

EXERCISE 4 WORKBOOK PAGE 77

Student Reader

Lesson 36 - Review

VOCABULARY:
check-in (to)	desk	receptionist	identify (to)	show (to)
peace	card	memorial	peaceful	hotel

ACTIVITY 1 Listen to the audio first.
Then take turns reading it orally with your teacher.
Divide into small groups. Role-play and then change roles.

https://tinyurl.com/2tymmjsa

Narrator: When Rose, Luke, Carol and Tom arrived at the hotel in Delhi, they went to the front desk to check-in.

Rose: We have a reservation for two rooms. The names are Smith and Jones.
Receptionist: Could I have some picture identification please?

Narrator: They gave the receptionist their picture identification cards.
Receptionist: Your rooms are on the second floor. Here are your keys. I will show you to your rooms.

Narrator: The two couples put their bags in their rooms, and went down to the restaurant to get some breakfast.

Tom: What do we want to do today?
Luke: I want to see Mahatma Gandhi's Memorial.
Carol: That's a good idea!

Tom: Let's go there.
Carol: We'll get a taxi.
Luke: Okay, let's go!

ACTIVITY 2 Look at the picture and work with your teacher to answer these questions.

1. Where is Mahatma Gandhi's Memorial? (India)

2. Did you go to Gandhi's Memorial last year?

3. Did Gandhi work for peace?

4. Does the Memorial have a garden?

EXERCISE 1	WORKBOOK PAGE 78
EXERCISE 2	WORKBOOK PAGE 78

Student Reader

64

LESSON 36 CONTINUED

ACTIVITY 3 Divide into groups of two or three. Ask and answer in sentences.

1. Are you drinking juice now?
2. Did you arrive here ten minutes ago?
3. Did you study English last year?
4. Did you see your neighbor last night?
5. Were you eating breakfast an hour ago?
6. Are you learning English now?
7. Is your friend working now?
8. Are you speaking now?
9. Did you buy something the day before yesterday?
10. Were you reading a book last night?
11. Do you want to see Gandhi's Memorial?

https://tinyurl.com/2p99bcar

1. Yes, I'm drinking juice now.
   No, I'm not drinking juice now.
2. Yes, I arrived (here) ten minutes ago.
   No, I didn't arrive (here) ten minutes ago.
3. Yes, I studied English last year.
   No, I didn't study English last year.
4. Yes, I saw my neighbor last night.
   No, I didn't see my neighbor last night.
5. Yes, I was eating breakfast an hour ago.
   No, I wasn't eating breakfast an hour ago.
6. Yes, I'm learning English now?
   No, I'm not learning English now.
7. Yes, my friend is working now.
   No, my friend isn't working now.
8. Yes, I'm speaking now.
   No, I'm not speaking now.
9. Yes, I bought something the day before yesterday.
   No, I didn't buy anything the day before yesterday.
10. Yes, I was reading a book last night.
    No, I wasn't reading a book last night.
11. Yes, I want to see Gandhi's Memorial.
    No, I don't want to see Gandhi's Memorial.

EXERCISE 3 WORKBOOK PAGE 79   TEST 9 GUIDE PAGES 132-133

Student Reader

Lesson 37

VOCABULARY:

quarter	half	tell (to)	clock	outline	tonight
next	garden	plan (to)	brochure	o'clock	tire (to)

NOTE: You will see AM or PM after a time.
10 AM = ten o'clock in the morning.
10 PM = ten o'clock in the evening.

A STUDENT'S REFERENCE OUTLINE OF CLOCK TIMES

ten past ten   a quarter past ten   twenty past ten   half past ten   twenty to ten   a quarter to eleven

OR

ten ten   ten fifteen   ten twenty   ten thirty   ten forty   ten forty-five

We use clock times when talking about something that happened in the past or in the future.
In Lesson 35 the simple future tense using "will" was introduced.
There is a second way of talking about the simple future.

I'<u>m going to swim</u> tomorrow.
Use: to be + going + the infinitive = **<u>am going to swim</u>**

Singular: (am, is, are) <u>going to</u> _____   **Plural**

I am going to hike up the mountain.   *We are going to hike* up the mountain.
You are going to hike up the mountain.   *You are going to hike* up the mountain.
He is going to hike up the mountain.   *They are going to hike* up the mountain.
She is going to hike up the mountain.
It is going to hike up the mountain.

ORAL QUESTIONS   TEACHER'S GUIDE

EXERCISES 1, 2   WORKBOOK PAGE 80
EXERCISES 3 4   WORKBOOK PAGE 81
ACTIVITY 3   GUIDE PAGES 136-137

Student Reader

Lesson 37 Continued

ACTIVITY 1 Listen to your teacher read the dialogue.
Divide into small groups and role-play it three or four times.

Narrator: Rose, Luke, Carol and Tom had a good time visiting Mahatma Gandhi's Memorial, where they read about Gandhi and enjoyed the peaceful garden.
Sitting at breakfast in the hotel the next morning, they planned their last day in Delhi.

Carol: What are we going to do today?

Rose: There are some free brochures on the desk. I'll get one.

Luke: Good idea.

Tom: Let's go to Connaught Place.

Carol: What can we do there?

Rose: This brochure about Connaught Place says there are many stores and restaurants.

Luke: Let's go to the Lotus Temple.

Tom: We can go to Connaught Place this morning and to the Lotus Temple this afternoon.

Carol: I like that idea!

Luke: That's great!

Tom: We're going to get the bus home at six o'clock tonight.

Rose: We're going to be tired. We are going to be sleeping on the bus!

Carol: We'll have twelve hours to sleep!

Carol

Rose

Tom

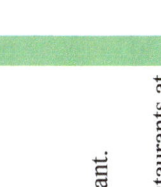
Luke

ACTIVITY 2 Ask each other:

1. Where did the two couples go in Delhi yesterday?
2. What did they read about?
3. Where are they sitting the next morning?
4. What did the brochure about Connaught place say?
5. Where are they going to go in the morning?
6. Where are they going to go in the afternoon?
7. When are they going to get the bus home?
8. What are they going to do on the bus home?
9. How many hours are they going to sleep?

1. They went to Mahatma Gandhi's Memorial.
2. They read about Gandhi.
3. They're sitting in the hotel restaurant.
4. It said there are many stores and restaurants at Connaught Place.
5. They're going to go to Connaught Place.
6. They're going to go to the Lotus Temple.
7. They're going to get the bus home at six o'clock.
8. They're going to be sleeping.
9. They're going to sleep for twelve hours.

Student Reader

LESSON 38

VOCABULARY:

hospital	taxi	word order	weekday	start (to)
Post Office	travel (to)	leg	transportation	bicycle
snowshoes	roller-blades	horseback	homemaker	skis

TRANSPORTATION

by train

by bus

by plane

by motorcycle

by bicycle

by boat

by car

PRESENT TENSE:
(If you are already there, use "come")

Do you <u>go</u> to Delhi by train?	No, I <u>go</u> by bus.
Do you <u>get</u> here by train?	No, I <u>get here</u> by car.
Do you <u>come</u> to class by train?	No, I <u>come</u> on foot.

PAST TENSE:

Did you <u>go</u> to Delhi by train?	No, I <u>went</u> by bus.
Did you <u>get</u> here by train?	No, I <u>got here</u> by car.
Did you <u>come</u> to class by train?	No, I <u>came</u> by car.

ACTIVITY 1   **WHOLE CLASS ACTIVITY**

Work with your teacher to answer these questions orally.

1. Craig goes to the bus stop. How is he going to travel?

2. Ruth and Nancy want a taxi. How are they going to travel?

3. Raymond and Ming want to fly to Delhi. How are they going to travel?

4. Peter and Sarah want to go across a lake. How are they going to travel?

5. Jessica goes to see her neighbor. How is she going to travel?

Student Reader

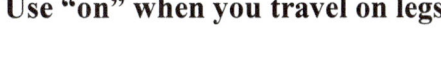

Lesson 38 Continued

Use "on" when you travel on legs.

on foot

on skis

on snowshoes

on horseback

on roller-blades

ORAL QUESTIONS   TEACHER'S GUIDE

ACTIVITY 2: Divide into small groups. Ask and answer the questions and read the answers.

1. How did you come to class today?
2. How are you going to get home this afternoon?
3. How did you travel to work?
4. How do you get to the movies?
5. How can you get to another country?
6. How do you travel through the snow?
7. How do you get to town?

I came to class on foot.
I came to class by bicycle / by motorcycle…
I'm going to get home on foot…
I'm going to get home by taxi / by bus…
I traveled on foot.
I traveled by bus.
I get to the movies by bus / on foot / by car.
I can get to another country by plane / by car / by train
I travel through the snow on foot / on snowshoes…
I get to town on foot.
I get to town by motorcycle / by bus

WORKBOOK - EXERCISES 1, 2 AND 3 PAGE 82
WORKBOOK – EXERCISES 4 AND 5 PAGE 83
WORKBOOK – ACTIVITY 3 PAGE 84

GUIDE – BINGO ANSWERS PAGE 139

Student Reader

Lesson 39 - Review

VOCABULARY:
- favorite
- policeman
- taxi driver
- head
- teacher
- mechanic
- hobby
- nurse
- artist
- doctor
- actress

ACTIVITY 1

Use the vocabulary words to complete the sentences orally:

She is a …

He is a …

He is an …

He is a …

He is a …

He is a …

ORAL QUESTIONS — TEACHER'S GUIDE

EXERCISE 1 - WORKBOOK PAGE 85
ACTIVITY 2 - WORKBOOK PAGE 86 AND GUIDE PAGES 142–143
ACTIVITY 3 - TEACHER'S GUIDE PAGE 141

Student Reader

LESSON 40

GO TO THE TEACHER'S GUIDE FOR THE FINAL TEST. PAGES 144-147

BEGINNERS ESL LESSON PLANS BOOK 2

STUDENT WORKBOOK

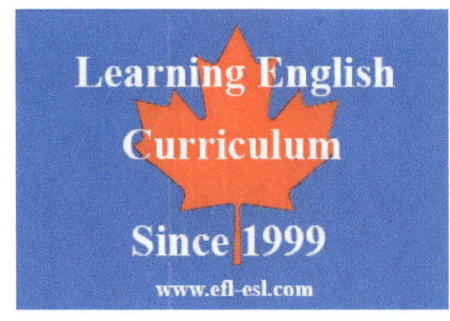

Student Reader

Book 2

STUDENT WORKBOOK

Student Reader

Lesson 21

EXERCISE 1

Do <u>not</u> use "the" before a name. **EXAMPLE:** He is in Pierre's Restaurant.
Use "the" when it is specific. **EXAMPLE:** <u>The</u> Church is on Pine Street.

1. How do Ruth and Raymond get to school?

_____

2. Where is the school?

_____

3. What is across from the park?

_____

4. Where is the supermarket?

_____

THE USE OF "ANY"

EXAMPLES: To ask a question when the answer is <u>singular</u>:
Do you have <u>a</u> hamburger? Yes, I have <u>a</u> hamburger. No, I don't have <u>a</u> hamburger.

To ask a question when the answer is <u>plural</u>:
How many hamburgers do you have? I have <u>six</u> hamburgers. I don't have <u>any</u> hamburgers.
Do you have some hamburgers? I have <u>some</u> hamburgers. I don't have <u>any</u> hamburgers.

ACTIVITY 3   Ask your partner.   Answer in sentences Use reported speech.
PLURAL - SOME / ANY

1. Do you have some cats? (no)

_____

2. Do you see some hands? (yes)

_____

3. Do you see some dishes? (no)

_____

4. Do you have some apples? (no

_____

5. Do you see a church? (no

_____

6. Do you see some flowers? (yes)

_____

7. Do you have some matches? (no)

_____

8. Do you have some books? (yes)

_____

Student Reader

Lesson 21 Continued

EXERCISE 2   Answer the following questions in the positive and the negative:

EXAMPLE: I have ten flowers.   I don't have any flowers.

1. How many pens do you have?

(Positive) _____

(Negative) _____

2. How many dogs do you have?

(Positive) _____

(Negative) _____

EXERCISE 3   Answer in sentences

EXAMPLE: Where are the windows?   They are on the left.

1. Who is sitting across from you?

_____

2. Who is on your right?

_____

3. Do you sometimes walk along the street?

_____

4. Who is on your left?

_____

5. Do you get apples at the supermarket?

_____

6. Do you live across from a hospital?

_____

7. Is there a park in your town?

_____

8. Do you go to the theater?

_____

9. Is the school across from the Carter's house?

_____

Student Reader

LESSON 21 CONTINUED

ACTIVITY 3: (See Guide page 73 of Book 1 Part 1 for instructions about how to play.)

LIST 1 WORDS TO WRITE IN THE BINGO SQUARES:

my (mine)	theater	our (ours)	supermarket	Canadian
outside	his	house	hat	behind
here	boy	to come	grandfather	good
chair	dictionary	**1 corner**	Vancouver	left
to like	restaurant	can't	don't	

LIST 2 WORDS TO CALL

1. where you turn on the street
2. belongs to me
3. to enjoy.
4. where you buy things
5. opposite of in front of.
6. opposite of <u>there</u>
7. a mother's son.
8. opposite of right
9. belongs to us
10. opposite of <u>to go</u>
11. you eat there
12. opposite of do
13. you put it on your head
14. you see a movie there
15. you sit on it
16. opposite of bad
17. home
18. a nationality
19. belongs to him
20. a city
21. opposite of can
22. a book full of words
23. not inside
24. your father's father

BINGO
FREE

Student Reader

LESSON 22

EXERCISE 1 Answer the questions in sentences.
NOTE: Use the preposition <u>on</u> for <u>specific days</u> of the week.

1. When do Raymond's parents go to the church?
   _____

2. What does Ruth like to do?
   _____

3. Who works as a volunteer with Ruth?
   _____

4. When do they volunteer at the hospital?
   _____

5. What do they sometimes buy on the way home?
   _____

6. What do Raymond and his friend do?
   _____

7. When do they hike?
   _____

8. What volunteer work do they do?
   _____

9. What do they often buy on the way home?
   _____

10. Do you do volunteer work?
    _____

EXERCISE 2

Put these sentences into the <u>singular</u>. **EXAMPLE:** The curtains are at (on) the windows.
The curtain is at (on) the window.

1. They have four neighbors.   _____

2. There are six friends here.   _____

3. There are five stores.   _____

4. The streets have many dogs.   _____

5. There are some churches.   _____

6. The cities have many restaurants.   _____

Student Reader

Lesson 22 Continued - Review

SINGULAR AND PLURAL

EXERCISE 3 Put the following sentences into the plural.

EXAMPLE: The book is on the table.   The books are on the tables.

1. He is a student. _____

2. I have a dog. _____

3. She has a glass. _____

4. He is from Australia. _____

5. There is a mountain beside the city. _____
_____

6. She meets a friend. _____
_____

EXERCISE 4 REVIEW OF PREPOSITIONS

Fill in the missing words, using: on   from   at   a
(Each word may be used more than once.)

Raymond Carter is _____ Australian. He lives with his family _____ 11 Kent Street. His sister is Ruth. She lives _____ home with her family _____ Kent Street.

Raymond's neighbor is Ming. His mother and father are _____ China, but they are Australians now. Ming lives _____ 13 Kent Street. Raymond and Ming are friends.

Nancy is Ming's neighbor. She is Ruth's friend, too. Nancy lives _____ 15 Kent Street. She lives in an apartment _____ the third floor. Ming, Nancy, Raymond and Ruth are neighbors. They all live _____ Kent Street.

Student Reader

LESSON 23

https://tinyurl.com/2s429hkp

EXERCISE 1   Answer the questions in sentences.

1. Where are Peter and Sarah?_____

2. Is the snow deep there? _____

3. Is it cold there? _____

4. What is the snow like? _____

5. Can Peter walk through deep snow? _____

6. Do you climb mountains? _____

7. Why does Sarah want to climb to the top of the mountain?

_____

8. Do they keep climbing?_____

9. Does Peter have a warm hat? _____

10. Does Peter follow Sarah?_____

EXERCISE 2:   **MATCH THE MEANING**

clothes   _____

snow   _____

sure   _____

cannot   _____

to head   _____

warm   _____

trail   _____

supper   _____

| you wear them | not too hot or too cold | you eat it | yes |
| to go | a small road | can't | it's very cold |

Student Reader

Lesson 23 Continued

EXERCISE 3

1. Where are you?

   _____

2. Where do you live? (street and number)

   _____

3. Where are the windows?

   _____

4. Where is the door?

   _____

5. How many students are in the classroom?

   _____

   Look at the map on page 39.
6. How do you go from the Tibetan Restaurant to the hospital?

   _____

   _____

7. Where is the supermarket?

   _____

8. The book is Mary's. Whose book is it? (use a possessive pronoun)

   _____

9. The dog belongs to you. Whose dog is it? (use a possessive pronoun)

   _____

10. The house belongs to Craig and Jessica.
    Whose house is it? (use a possessive pronoun)

    _____

11. The desks belong to us. Whose desks are they? (use a possessive pronoun)

    _____

12. The clothes belong to James.
    Whose clothes are they? (use a possessive pronoun)

    _____

    _____

Student Workbook

Lesson 23 Continued

ACTIVITY 3: Divide into groups of two or three.
Ask each other these questions. Write the answers.

EXAMPLE: Can the dog get the book?   No, the dog can't get the book.

1. Is the dog on the table?
   _____

2. Where is the book?
   _____

3. What is between the lamp and the table?
   _____

4. Is the lamp beside the table
   _____

5. Is the dog beside the table?
   _____

6. Is the dog under the table?
   _____

7. Are there two books on the table?
   _____

8. Where is the dog?
   _____

9. Is the book under the table?
   _____

10. Do you have a dog under your desk?
    _____

Student Workbook

Lesson 24

EXERCISE 1

MATCH THE MEANING
Write the meaning beside the word.
one - first

EXAMPLE:

neighbors _____   floor _____   sure _____

home _____   a chair _____   great _____

a friend _____   movie _____   lunch _____

dictionary _____   to stretch _____

your desk is on it   where you live   someone you like   you sit on it
you live beside them   very good   it has words in it   you eat it at 12:00
you see it in a theatre   yes   to extend from place to place

EXERCISE 2 — ANSWER IN SENTENCES

1. Do you have a cat under your table?
   _____

2. Where does your neighbor live?
   _____

3. What is outside your window?
   _____

4. Do you drink water?
   _____

5. What is in your hand?
   _____

6. Are you at your home now?
   _____

7. Do you live on the fifteenth floor?
   _____

8. Do you hike in the mountains?
   _____

9. How many students are here?
   _____

10. Do you volunteer on Sundays?
    _____

Student Workbook

Lesson 24 Continued

ACTIVITY 3 ASK YOUR PARTNER.
Use a/ an the or some in some of your answers.
Use any for plural negative answers. Use reported speech.

EXAMPLE: Do you have some cats?

Yes, he/she has some cats.   No, he/she doesn't have any cats.

https://tinyurl.com/muxb6bbe

Use "a / an, the" or "some" in your answers.
Use "any" for plural negative answers.

1. Do you have some dogs?
   _____

2. Do you have some lamps?
   _____

3. Do you have some cats?
   _____

4. Do you have a book?
   _____

5. Do you have some pencils?
   _____

6. Do you have a sister?
   _____

EXERCISE 3 Use these words to complete the sentences.

| town | cold | eat | hike | small |
| deep | mountain | warm | beautiful | |

Sarah and Peter _____ through the snow. As they go up the _____

the snow gets deeper. It is _____ up there but they have _____ clothes.

When they look down they can see their _____ below. It looks very _____

from up there. The snow is _____ at the top of the mountain. They can see the

_____ snowy mountains that stretch on and on. They decide to enjoy them

and have something to _____.

Student Workbook   52

LESSON 24 CONTINUED

EXERCISE 4

Look at the dialogue on Page 44. Answer these questions in sentences.

1. Where are Sarah and Peter?

2. Can they see the town below?

3. How does the town look?

4. Can they see the building where they live?

5. Where is their building?

6. What is the snow like at the top of the mountain?

7. Do they get to the top of the mountain?

8. What do they see on the other side of the mountain?

9. Do you live beside a mountain?

10. Who has a good idea?

11. What is her good idea?

Do you clmb mountains?

Student Workbook

LESSON 25

EXERCISE 1:   Write the past tense of these **regular verbs**.

to need   _____

to watch   _____

to phone   _____

to play   _____

to close   _____

to follow   _____

to look   _____

to decide   _____

to correct   _____

EXERCISE 2

The verb "to do" is not a regular verb.   Write the past tense of "to do".   _____

Write the negative past tense contraction of "to do". _____

EXERCISE 3   **Answer in sentences using the past tense.**

1. Did you play basketball last night? (yes)

_____

2. Did you watch television last night? (yes)

_____

3. Did you live in the India last year? (yes)

_____

4. Did your friends play basketball yesterday? (yes)

_____

5. Did you like the theater last night? (yes)

_____

6. Did you walk to class today? (yes)

_____

7. Did you hike up the mountain yesterday? (yes)

_____

Student Workbook

Lesson 25 Continued

EXERCISE 4

Put the words in the right order.

1. friend, I, phoned, my

2. the, She, door, closed

3. watch, liked, They, the

4. Russia, He, in, lived

5. asked, play, to, basketball, They

6. her, dogs, followed, The

7. afternoon, enjoyed, We, the

8. the, He, phone, answered

EXERCISE 5

MATCH THE MEANING

to watch _____

to do _____

year _____

weekend _____

to follow _____

to stretch _____

food _____

small _____

machine _____

to go behind something	Saturday and Sunday	365 days	did	to extend
you make it work for you	what you eat	not big		to look for a long time

Student Workbook

55

Lesson 26

EXERCISE 1 Find the past tense verbs in the paragraph on Page 48 of the student Book. Write them below and write the correct infinitive beside them.
EXAMPLE: went – to go

_____   _____   _____   _____

_____   _____   _____   _____

EXERCISE 2   Answer these questions using the past tense.
EXAMPLE: When <u>did</u> the Carters go to town?   They <u>went</u> to town on Saturdays.

1. Where did Craig Carter go?

2. What did Jessica find in the library?

3. Where did Ruth see good CD's?

4. Where did Raymond meet his friends?

5. What did they sometimes buy for supper?

ACTIVITY 3   Ask your friends the following questions. Use reported speech.
EXAMPLE: Did you watch television last night?   Yes, (he/she) <u>watched</u> television last night.
                                                     No, (he/she) <u>didn't watch</u> television last night.

1. Did you come to class yesterday? *(come - came)*

2. Did you go to a restaurant yesterday? *(go - went)*

3. Did you meet your friend last night? *(meet - met)*

4. Did you eat lunch today? *(eat - ate)*

5. Did you buy a hat last week? *(buy - bought)*

6. Did you write to your friend last night? *(write - wrote)*

7. Did you find your watch? *(find – found)*

Student Workbook

Lesson 26 Continued

EXERCISE 3   **MATCH THE MEANING**

a ticket _____

library _____

a movie _____

a song _____

road _____

Saturday _____

afternoon _____

the latest _____

a day of the week   cars drive on it   the time after lunch
you get books there   you watch it   you listen to it
you buy it for a movie or a bus   the newest   saw
went   had

Match the past tense of these verbs.

to go _____

to have _____

to see _____

EXERCISE 4   Fill in the blanks using the past tense of the verbs.
What did the Carters do on Saturdays last month?

Last month the Carters _____ (to do) many things on Saturdays. Craig _____ (to go) to the video store. Jessica usually _____ (to look) for good books in the library.

Ruth _____ (to like) to find good CD's in the music store. She often _____ (to listen) with her friend Nancy. They _____ (to enjoy) learning the latest songs.

On Saturday afternoon Raymond usually _____ (to meet) many of his friends outside the theater. Sometimes they _____ (to buy) tickets to see the movie. After the movie they _____ (to walk) along the road to buy pizza.

Student Workbook

Lesson 26 Continued

ACTIVITY 4: (See Guide page 73 of Book 1 Part 1 for instructions about how to play.

Write the numbers of the words in LIST 1 beside the word or phrase that means the same in LIST 2. Number 1 has been done for you.

BINGO
WRITE THESE WORDS

LIST 1

1 store	7 library	13 pizza	19 town
2 to sit	8 to eat	14 to begin	20 to buy
3 a song	9 a letter	15 a door	21 a restaurant
4 home	10 lunch	16 a theater	22 a chair
5 a friend	11 neighbors	17 to find	23 to write
6 to hike	12 to study	18 to come	24 to meet

LIST 2   CALL THESE WORDS

	wrote	sat	ate
1	where you buy something	you find books there	you eat it
	where the stores are	you listen to it	you write it
	began	bought	hiked
	you can close it	you can eat there	where you live
	studied	came	met
	you eat it at 12:00	you enjoy music there	you sit on it
	a person you like	you live beside them	found

		BINGO FREE		

Student Workbook

LESSON 27

EXERCISE 1   Answer in sentences. Use the past tense.

1. Where were you last night?
   _____

2. Were you in town yesterday?
   _____

3. Were you in front of the school today?
   _____

4. Was your friend in town yesterday?
   _____

5. Was your friend at home last week?
   _____

6. Was your dog at home this morning?
   _____

7. Was your cat inside last night?
   _____

8. Were you in the supermarket yesterday?
   _____

ACTIVITY 2

ASK TWO OTHER STUDENTS   INFORMATION SHEET   ANSWER IN SENTENCES

STUDENT 1

What was your name last year?   _____

How old were you last year?   _____

What was your hobby last year?   _____

Who were your friends last year?   _____

STUDENT 2

What was your name last year?   _____

How old were you last year?   _____

What was your hobby last year?   _____

Who were your friends last year?   _____

Student Workbook

Lesson 27 Continued

EXERCISE 2

Look at each picture and write the answers to the question:

1. Where were you yesterday? _____
   _____

2. Was it cold outside this morning?
   _____
   _____

Look at each picture and complete the question. Then answer the question.

3. Were you at _____ yesterday?
   _____
   _____

4. Were you at the _____ last night?
   _____
   _____

5. Were many people in the _____ yesterday afternoon?
   _____
   _____

6. Were you in a _____ last night?
   _____
   _____

7. Were you hiking in the _____ last weekend?
   _____
   _____

Student Workbook

Lesson 28 - Review

EXERCISE 1

See the Student Reader map on Page 39.
Complete using these words. Each word may be used more than once.

| from | in | to | along | at | on |

The Carters live (1) _____ Kent Street (2) _____ number 11. Raymond and Ruth walk (3) _____ Wilson Street (4) _____ their school. They walk two blocks to school. To go to the supermarket, they walk (5) _____ Kent Street to West Street, they turn right and walk two blocks. The stores are (6) _____ the right.

EXERCISE 2   Answer these questions in sentences.

1. Do you have three rings?
   _____

2. How many books do you have?
   _____

3. How many elephants do you have?
   _____

4. Where do you go after class?
   _____

5. Do you go to town on Saturdays?
   _____

6. Did you play basketball last year?
   _____

7. Did you eat supper at home yesterday?
   _____

8. Did you hike in the mountains last year?
   _____

9. Were you at the theater last night?
   _____

10. Was your friend at your house last night?
    _____

Student Workbook

Lesson 29

ACTIVITY 2 Ask a partner the questions and write the answers. Use reported speech.

EXAMPLE: When did you swim?   He / She swam last weekend.

1. When did you walk to town?
   _____

2. When did you see your neighbor?
   _____

3. When did you buy a book?
   _____

4. When did you attend a theater?
   _____

5. When did you begin English classes?
   _____

6. When did you walk through town?
   _____

7. When did you phone your friend?
   _____

8. When did you eat in a restaurant?
   _____

9. When did you study English?
   _____

EXERCISE 1 Make sentences putting the following words in the correct order.

1. breakfast, He, today, cooked.

2. wrote, a, yesterday, letter, They

3. Saturdays, hike, They, on

4. TV, night, They, last, watched

5. book, She, minute, a, closed, ago, the

6. followed, That, today, dog, them, home

Student Workbook

Lesson 29 Continued

EXERCISE 2   ANSWER IN SENTENCES

1. Did you come to class the day before yesterday?
   _____

2. Did you study English a year ago?
   _____

3. Did you eat breakfast three hours ago?
   _____

4. Did you visit your friend the day before yesterday?
   _____

5. Did you talk to a student ten minutes ago?
   _____

6. What day was it the day before yesterday?
   _____

7. Did you phone your friend twenty-four hours ago?
   _____

8. Did you eat in a restaurant the day before yesterday?
   _____

9. Are the stores closed on Sundays?
   _____

ACTIVITY 3   BINGO
(See Guide page 73 of Book 1 Part 1 for instructions about how to play.)

MATCH THE PAST TENSE WITH THE INFINITIVE OF THE VERB

INFINITIVES TO PRINT					
to find	to attend	to begin	to come	to do	to go
to have	to live	to meet	to see	to sit	to put
to buy	to eat	to want	to study	to volunteer	to play
to follow	to answer	to enjoy	to hike	to run	to like

PAST TENSE VERBS TO CALL					
wanted	ate	ran	bought	volunteered	saw
studied	sat	put	hiked	played	met
lived	liked	had	went	enjoyed	did
came	began	attended	followed	answered	

Student Workbook   63

Lesson 29 Continued

		BINGO FREE		

		BINGO FREE		

Student Workbook

Lesson 30

EXERCISE 1   Present Progressive Tense   He is playing soccer now.

1. What is he doing now?
   _____

2. Are you playing soccer now?
   _____

3. What are you doing now?
   _____

4. What is your friend doing now?
   _____

EXERCISE 2   Complete the sentences by adding "ing" to the words in (brackets).

1. He is _____ her every day. (phone)
2. They are _____ on Saturdays. (hike)
3. They are _____ soccer now. (practice)
4. The man was _____ them. (watch)
5. He is _____ a dictionary. (use)
6. She is _____ a letter. (write)
7. They are _____ some volunteer work. (do)

EXERCISE 3   Add –ing to the word in (brackets) to complete the sentence.

1. She is _____ to sew. (try)
2. They are _____ all night with their friends. (party)
3. They are _____ the fish. (fry)
4. The friends are _____ the beach. (enjoy)
5. The students are _____ English. (study)
6. The plane is _____ to Bombay. (fly)
7. He is _____. (cry)
8. They enjoy _____ soccer. (play)

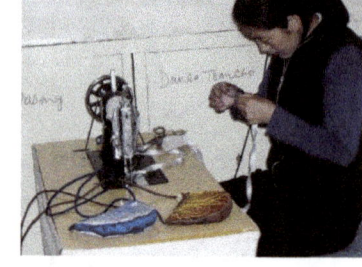

Student Workbook

Lesson 30 Continued

EXERCISE 4 Change these sentences from the present tense to the present progressive.

EXAMPLE: Ruth plays basketball.   Ruth is playing basketball.

1. Nancy eats breakfast. _____
2. Ming has Chinese food for dinner. _____
3. Raymond rides a bicycle. _____
4. Craig cooks supper. _____
5. It rains outside. _____
6. Jessica enjoys the snow. _____
7. Ruth reads a book. _____
8. I study English now. _____
9. Nancy wears a pair of gloves. _____

REVIEW ACTIVITY 1:   FIND A PARTNER: ASK EACH OTHER:
USE YOUR PARTNER'S NAME. EXAMPLE: <u>Marie</u> is from _____.

1. Where are you from? _____
2. How many faces do you have? _____
3. Do you have a dress? _____
4. Are you from Canada? _____
5. What is in front of you? _____
6. When did you come to class? (time) _____
7. Where is your house? (street name) _____
8. Who is with you? _____
9. When do you come to English classes? _____
10. Where do you live? (name + number) _____
11. Did you walk to class today? _____

EXERCISE 5   Answer these questions in sentences.

1. Where is Peter?   3. How does Sarah look?

   _____   _____

2. How is Peter?   4. Do you like Chinese food?

   _____   _____

Lesson 31

SPELLING

Spelling one-syllable words with ING or ED.

<u>One vowel and two consonants:</u>   sit + t + ing = sitting   stop + p + ed = stopped

EXERCISE 1   Add <u>ing</u> to these words:

put _____   swim _____   stop _____

<u>Two vowels and one consonant:</u>   meet + ing = meeting   look + ed = looked

EXERCISE 2   Add <u>ing</u> to these words:

eat _____   wear _____

cook _____   rain _____

EXERCISE 3   Add -ed to these words:

cook _____   look _____   rain _____

EXERCISE 4   Complete the sentences using "ing" or "ed"

1. It is _____ outside. (rain)
2. He is _____ dinner. (cook)
3. It _____ yesterday. (rain)
4. She is _____ her friend. (meet)
5. They are _____ at the table. (sit)
6. She is _____ her book on the table. (put)
7. He is _____ at the corner. (stop)
8. She is _____ in the water. (swim)
9. They are _____ their friends. (meet)
10. Are you _____ a coat? (wear)
11. The car _____ at the corner. (stop)

NOTE: When the verb ends in a <u>silent single "e"</u>, drop the "e" before adding "ing" (live - living)

EXERCISE 5   Add "ing" to these verbs:

use _____   write _____   ride _____   have _____

come _____   phone _____   close _____   arrive _____

Student Workbook

Lesson 31 Continued

EXERCISE 6 Answer these questions using the present progressive tense.

1. Are you practicing basketball now?
   _____

2. Are you reading a book?
   _____

3. Is your mother living in this city?
   _____

4. Are you wearing a T-shirt today?
   _____

5. Are you talking to a friend?
   _____

6. Are you eating dinner?
   _____

EXERCISE 7 Make sentences using all of these words.

1. are, classroom, the, We, in   _____
2. the, He, radio, listens, to   _____
3. go, They, work, to   _____
4. wearing, jeans, He, blue, is   _____
5. fish, are, They, frying, a   _____
6. arrived, day, yesterday, the, They, before   _____
7. She, ten, ate, minutes, breakfast, ago   _____
8. wasn't, at, She, home   _____
9. laughing, He, was   _____
10. in, She, wrote, notebook, her   _____

Student Workbook

Lesson 31 Continued

ACTIVITY 3   **BINGO**

FIRST: Write the number from LIST 2 beside the word(s) it describes in LIST 1.
EXAMPLE: 1 - weekend
SECOND: Write the words from LIST 1 into the Bingo squares.
THIRD: Play the game.

MATCH THE MEANING
LIST 1: WRITE THESE WORDS IN THE SQUARES

lunch	to stop	to sleep	sure
days off	a pair of shoes	notebook	work
a pair of gloves	Chinese food	television	feet
a plane (airplane)	a fish	to fry	mango juice
1 weekend	a store	breakfast	an hour
inside	a library	pictures	a game

LIST 2:   CALL THESE PHRASES

1 Saturday and Sunday	9 people paint them	17 you fly in it
2 Chinese people cook it	10 it has many books	18 you do it at night
3 you wear them on your feet	11 you do it for money	19 60 minutes
4 days you don't go to work	12 you write in it	20 not outside
5 you eat it in the morning	13 where you buy something	21 yes
6 how you cook something	14 it lives in the water	22 you play it
7 you wear them on your hands	15 you eat it at 12:00	23 you watch it
8 you don't go / you don't walk	16 they're on your legs	24 you drink it

		BINGO FREE		

Student Workbook

Lesson 32

EXERCISE 1 Answer the questions in sentences:

1. Where do Craig and Jessica go on Friday nights?
   _____

2. Is Raymond practicing archery three times a week?
   _____

3. Is Ruth playing on a school team?
   _____

4. Where is Toto on Friday nights?
   _____

5. What is Toto doing?
   _____

6. Do you go to a restaurant on Friday nights?
   _____

EXERCISE 2 ANSWER IN THE <u>PRESENT PROGRESSIVE TENSE</u>

EXAMPLE: Are you playing soccer now?
Yes, I'm playing soccer now.
No, I'm not playing soccer now.

Are you watching television now?
_____

Are you eating lunch in a restaurant now?
_____

3. Is your friend looking out the window now?
   _____

4. What are you doing now?
   _____

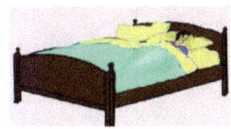

5. Are you sleeping now?
   _____

6. Are you drinking mango juice now?
   _____

Student Workbook

Lesson 32 Continued

EXERCISE 3

1. What is the boy doing?

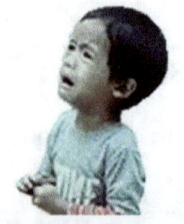

_____

2. What are they doing with the fish?

_____

3. What is she doing?

_____

4. What is he doing?

_____

5. What is he practicing?

_____

6. What are you practicing?

umbrella

_____

Student Workbook

Lesson 33

EXERCISE 1 Answer the questions in sentences.

1. What was Ruth doing yesterday morning?
   _____

2. Were you playing basketball last night?
   _____

3. What were you doing yesterday?
   _____

4. Was it snowing last week?
   _____

5. Were you practicing archery the day before yesterday?
   _____

EXERCISE 2 Change these sentences from the past tense to the past progressive.

EXAMPLE: Jack <u>watched</u> TV yesterday.   Jack <u>was watching</u> TV yesterday.

1. Craig drove his car to work last week.   _____

2. Ruth rode her bicycle to school today.   _____

3. Nancy bought a pair of shoes.   _____

4. Raymond wore a pair of gloves.   _____

5. Craig and Jessica went to a movie.   _____

6. Ming practiced soccer last week.   _____

7. They lived in Australia last year.   _____

8. She came to school.   _____

9. They hiked through the snow.   _____

10. They volunteered at the hospital.   _____

Student Workbook

Lesson 33 Continued

EXERCISE 3 ANSWER USING THE <u>PAST PROGRESSIVE TENSE</u>

1. Was your friend laughing this morning?
   _____

2. Were you wearing a jacket yesterday?
   _____

3. Was your teacher wearing a long dress this morning?
   _____

4. Were you eating an apple last night?
   _____

5. Were you walking through town yesterday afternoon?
   _____

ACTIVITY 3 PAST TENSE INFORMATION CARD
<u>Answer in sentences.</u>

What was your friend's name? _____

What was your friend's nationality? _____

What was your friend doing then? (activity) _____

When was your friend having his/her days off? _____

****

What was your friend's name? _____

What was your friend's nationality? _____

What was your friend doing then? (activity) _____

When was your friend having his/her days off? _____

Student Workbook

Lesson 34

EXERCISE 1 Answer the questions using these phrases.

*   in the morning   in the afternoon   in the evening
    at noon   at night   at midnight
    at breakfast   at lunch   at supper (at dinner)

EXAMPLE: When is it lunchtime in North America?   *It's lunchtime at noon.*
When do you do your homework?   *I do it in the evening.*
Put <u>when something happens</u> at the end of the sentence.

1. When do you eat breakfast? _____
2. When do you go to sleep? _____
3. When do you see your friends? _____
4. When do you eat dinner in San Francisco? _____
5. When do you go to work / school? _____
6. When do you eat lunch? _____
7. When do you sleep? _____

EXERCISE 2 Complete the following using these prepositions.

with   on   at

Raymond and his friend Ming did many things last year. They often hiked in the mountains

_____ Saturdays and they usually went to a lake to swim _____ Sundays.

Sometimes they went out _____ their friends to a restaurant. After dinner,

they returned home late _____ the evening and went to bed _____ midnight.

EXERCISE 3   **MATCH THE MEANING**

park   _____

breakfast   _____

music   _____

fly   _____

hungry   _____

shoes   _____

you wear them on your feet   you want something to eat   airplanes do it

a quiet place with many trees   you listen to it   you eat it in the morning

Student Workbook

Lesson 34 Continued

ACTIVITY 2 WHAT DID YOU DO LAST WEEK?

1. Answer these questions to complete the chart on this page.

	What did you do?	Where did you go?	When did you go?
EXAMPLE 1:	I swam.	I went to a lake.	I went on Sunday

2. Ask a friend. Use reported speech.

	What did you do?	Where did you go?	When did you go?
EXAMPLE 2:	He / She swam.	He / She went to a lake.	He / She went <u>on</u> Sunday.

What did you do?	Where did you go?	When did you go?
1.		
2.		

EXERCISE 4 Answer the following questions in sentences:

EXAMPLE: What day comes before Friday? Thursday comes before Friday.

1. What day comes after Tuesday? _____

2. What month comes after July? _____

3. What day comes after Sunday? _____

4. What are the last four months of the year? _____

5. When is your birthday? _____

6. In what month is Christmas? _____

7. When do you eat supper? _____

8. Do you like to get up in the morning? _____

9. Are you sometimes late for class? _____

10. Do you sleep late on Sunday mornings? _____

Student Workbook

Lesson 35

EXERCISE 1
EXAMPLE:

Write each sentence in the future tense.

Present	Future
I ride my bicycle.	I will ride my bicycle.

1. He plays soccer. _____
2. She drives the car to town. _____
3. They practice basketball. _____
4. They hike all day. _____
5. The boys eat chicken. _____
6. She wears a pair of gloves. _____
7. It rains outside. _____
8. She looks for a pair of shoes. _____
9. He begins English classes. _____
10. She knows the answer. _____

EXERCISE 2   Answer each question using the future tense.

1. Where will you go tomorrow?

   _____

2. When will you go to Delhi?

   _____

3. Where will you find your friend?

   _____

4. Who will you see tomorrow?

   _____

5. What will you see in the store?

   _____

6. Where will you eat breakfast?

   _____

Student Workbook

Lesson 35 Continued

MAKING QUESTIONS ABOUT THE FUTURE

Use a question word + will

What will you eat?
When will we eat?
Where will I eat?
How will I find the theatre?
Who will you see at school?
Which way will I go?

EXERCISE 3   Make questions using the following:
EXAMPLE: What / see   What will you see?

1. When / go   _____?

2. Where / live _____?

3. How / know   _____?

4. Who / meet   _____?

5. Where / hike _____?

6. Where / stay _____?

EXERCISE 4   Read the dialogue on Page 63 of the Student Reader.
Answer these questions in sentences.

1. Who wanted to have a holiday?
   _____

2. Will they go to Delhi?
   _____

3. How will they get to Delhi?
   _____

4. Where will they stay in Delhi?
   _____

5. Where will they meet?
   _____

6. Who will phone for a hotel reservation?
   _____

7. Which hotel will she phone?
   _____

Student Workbook

Lesson 36

EXERCISE 1 Answer these questions in sentences.

1. Where did the two couples go?

2. Where did they go to check-in?

3. What are their surnames?

4. Who gave them the keys to their rooms?

5. Where were their rooms?

6. Who showed them to their rooms?

7. Where did they eat breakfast?

8. What does Luke want to see??

9. How will they get to Gandhi's Memorial?

EXERCISE 2 **MATCH THE MEANING**

Sunday _____

March _____

December _____

Saturday and Sunday _____

February _____

July _____

April _____

Wednesday _____

the fourth month of the year   the middle of the week
the seventh month   the weekend
the first day of the week   the last month of the year
the second month of the year   the third month of the year

Student Workbook

Lesson 36 Continued

EXERCISE 3

1. **These paragraphs are in the present tense.**
Read them and underline the verb in each sentence.

Rose, Luke, Carol and Tom arrive at the Peace Hotel in Delhi. They go to the front desk to check-in. The receptionist asks them for their last names and for their picture identification cards. She says, "Thank you". She gives them keys to their rooms. Then she shows them the way to the second floor.

The two couples put their bags in their rooms. Then they go down to the restaurant for breakfast. They talk about Delhi. They decide to see Mahatma Gandhi's Memorial.

2. **Write these paragraphs in the future tense (will + verb), using the word in ( ) brackets.**

Rose, Luke, Carol, and Tom _____ (arrive) at the Peace Hotel in Delhi. They _____ (go) to the front desk to check-in. The receptionist _____ (ask) them for their last names and for their picture identification cards. She _____ (say) "Thank you". She _____ (give) them keys to their rooms. Then she _____ (show) them the way to the second floor.

The two couples _____ (put) their bags in their rooms. Then they _____ (go) down to the restaurant for breakfast. They _____ (talk) about Delhi. They _____ (decide) to see Mahatma Gandhi's Memorial.

Student Workbook

Lesson 37

EXERCISE 1 Change these sentences to the "going to" form of the simple future.

EXAMPLE: She eats breakfast at 8:00 AM.   She is going to eat breakfast at 8:00 AM.
We are going to eat breakfast at 8:00 AM.

1. They go to the mountains.   _____
2. They walk into the park.   _____
3. They drive to another city.   _____
4. He drinks mango juice.   _____
5. He looks for his car.   _____
6. She paints a picture.   _____
7. It will rain.   _____
8. They listen to the radio.   _____
9. They practice archery.   _____
10. He walks to town.   _____

EXERCISE 2 Making questions using question words + is/are + pronoun + going to

EXAMPLES:
<u>What</u> are you going to eat?
<u>When</u> is it going to be lunchtime?
<u>Where</u> are you going to eat?
<u>How</u> am I going to find the theater?
<u>Who</u> are you going to see at the party?

EXAMPLE: **What / see**   What are you going to see?

1. When / go   _____?
2. Where / live   _____?
3. How / know   _____?
4. Who / meet   _____?
5. What / ask   _____?

Student Workbook

Lesson 37 Continued

EXERCISE 3 MATCH THE MEANING

clock _____it tells the time_____

brochure _____

garden _____

a plan _____

hotel _____

desk _____

you sit at it   it tells about something   a place with beautiful trees
you sleep and eat there   it tells the time   it tells you what to do

EXERCISE 4 Answer these questions in sentences.

1. Are you going to leave home at half past eight?
   _____

2. Are you going to have tea with your friend at ten forty-five?
   _____

3. Are you going to help your friend tomorrow?
   _____

4. Are you going to go to your friend's party at nine fifteen?
   _____

5. Are you going to go to a church today?
   _____

6. Are you going to be at school tomorrow?
   _____

7. What are you going to do after dinner?
   _____

8. Are you going to be hiking in the mountains next week?
   _____

9. Are you going to visit a big city next year?
   _____

10. Are you going to bring some juice to the party?
    _____

Student Workbook

Lesson 38

EXERCISE 1 Answer these questions in sentences. Remember to use the right tense!

EXAMPLE: How did you get to town today?   I got <u>to town</u> on foot.   I got <u>there</u> on foot.

1. How do you come to class?
   _____

2. How do you get home from class?
   _____

3. Are you going to go to Bombay by plane?
   _____

4. Are you going to go to England by boat?
   _____

5. Are you going to go to work by bicycle?
   _____

6. Are you going to get married tomorrow?
   _____

EXERCISE 2 Use prepositions to complete these sentences.

Ruth went _____ town _____ 10:30 _____ Thursday. It was raining so

she went _____ car. She had _____ meet her friend Nancy _____ noon. Nancy

lives _____ Baker Street _____ another town. She came _____ train.

EXERCISE 3 Answer in sentences:

1. How did you come to class today?
   _____

2. How did you get to school / work two years ago?
   _____

3. Do you sometimes travel on skis?
   _____

4. How will you get to town tomorrow?
   _____

5. What is a good way to travel?
   _____

6. Do you like to travel by bus?
   _____

Student Workbook

Lesson 38 Continued

EXERCISE 4 FIND A PARTNER   ASK EACH OTHER

Use your partner's name or a pronoun when you answer in sentences.

EXAMPLE: How do you get to class?   Dawa gets to class by bus.   He gets to class by bus.

1. Did you come to class on skis?
   _____

2. Do you go to work by train?
   _____

3. Do you go to the Post Office on foot?
   _____

4. Did you come to class by car?
   _____

5. Did you go to another city by bus?
   _____

6. Do you get home by taxi?
   _____

7. Did you go to the hospital on horseback?
   _____

8. Can you go to work by boat?
   _____

EXERCISE 5 PRESENT PROGRESSIVE TENSE REVIEW.

Write these paragraphs in the present progressive tense (is / are + verb + ing).
Use the verb in ( ) brackets.

Rose, Luke, Carol and Tom _____ (arrive) at the Peace Hotel in Delhi. While they are standing at the front desk checking-in, the receptionist _____ (ask) them for their last names and for their picture identification cards. She says, "Thank you". After about five minutes she _____ (give) them the keys to their rooms and _____ (shows) them the way to the second floor.

The two couples put their bags in their rooms. Then they go down to the restaurant for breakfast. While they _____ (sit) at a table they _____ (talk) about Delhi. They _____ (decide) what they will do.

Student Workbook

Lesson 38 Continued

ACTIVITY 3   BINGO   PAST TENSE REVIEW

Write the numbers of the words in LIST 1 beside the word that means the same in LIST 2. Number 1 has been done for you.

LIST 1   WORDS TO PRINT:

1 to write	7 to answer	13 to arrive	19 to follow
2 to read	8 to attend	14 to travel	20 to want
3 to ride	9 to drive	15 to cook	21 to wear
4 to drink	10 to ask	16 to return	22 to happen
5 to tell	11 to use	17 to meet	23 to need
6 to start	12 to give	18 to work	24 to get

LIST 2   WORDS TO CALL:

gave	wrote	used	told
wore	cooked	answered	followed
worked	asked	returned	drank
wanted	rode	met	needed
started	happened	drove	attended
arrived	read	got	traveled

BINGO FREE

Student Workbook   84

Lesson 39 - Review

EXERCISE 1 Answer these questions in sentences.
Use the tense that is used in the question.

1. Were you eating lunch at eleven o'clock?
   _____

2. Do you walk outside in the morning?
   _____

3. What were you doing last night?
   _____

4. Is your teacher laughing now?
   _____

5. Were you writing a letter on the weekend?
   _____

6. Were you living in San Francisco last year?
   _____

7. Where do you wear your hat?
   _____

8. Do you usually listen to the radio on Sundays?
   _____

9. Were you wearing a T-shirt this morning?
   _____

10. Is it going to rain?
    _____

11. Were you sleeping at eight o'clock last night?
    _____

12. Were you walking in the park on the weekend?
    _____

Student Workbook

Lesson 39 Continued

ACTIVITY 2

Move about the class asking two students these questions
and answering those of others in sentences.
Use the information on your role-card.
Use reported speech.

NOTE: Use "**in**" before the name of a month. **EXAMPLE:** My last holiday was **in April**.

Ask two students these questions. **Write the answers in sentences**

What is your name? _____

How are you? _____

What is your occupation? _____

Are you married? _____

What is your favorite drink? _____

What is your favorite hobby? _____

What are you going to do on Saturday? _____

When do you get up in the morning? _____

When did you have your last holiday? _____

What is your name? _____

How are you? _____

What is your occupation? _____

Are you married? _____

What is your favorite drink? _____

What is your favorite hobby? _____

What are you going to do on Saturday? _____

When do you get up in the morning? _____

When did you have your last holiday? _____

Student Workbook

GLOSSARY

ENGLISH	NOTES	ENGLISH	NOTES
about		breakfast	
across from		bridge	
actress		bring (to), brought	
address		brochure	
adjective		brother	
after		brown	
afternoon		building	
ago		bus	
all		but	
along		buy (to), bought	
also		can	
and		cannot (can't)	
another		car	
answer (to), answered		card	
any		carpet maker	
anyone		cat	
anything		chair	
apartment		check-in (to), checked-in	
apple		Cheers!	
archery		chicken	
arrive (to), arrived		Chinese food	
artist		church	
ask (to), asked		city	
at home		class	
attend (to), attended		classmate	
bad		classroom	
basketball		clock	
be (to), am, is, are		close (to), closed	
beautiful		clothes	
bed		coffee	
before		cold	
begin (to), began		come (to), came	
behind		comfortable	
belong (to), belonged		computer	
below		consonant	
beside		cook (to), cooked	
big		corner	
bird		correct (to), corrected	
block		country	
blouse		couple	
blue jeans		cry (to), cried	
both		cup of tea	
box (boxes)		curtain	
boy		daughter	

Student Workbook

GLOSSARY

ENGLISH	NOTES	ENGLISH	NOTES
day-off		grandfather	
decide (to), decided		grandmother	
deep		great	
desk		hamburger	
dialogue		hand	
dictionary		handle	
dinner		hat	
dish		have (to), had	
do (to), did		hello	
doctor		her	
dog		here's	
donkey		Hi	
door		his	
dress		history	
dress (to), dressed		hot	
drink (to), drank		house	
drive (to), drove		how about…?	
each		how many	
eat (to), ate		husband	
enjoy (to), enjoyed		idea	
evening		in	
every		in front of	
face		interesting	
family		iron	
father		its	
find (to), found		jacket	
fine		juice	
first		just	
floor		know (to), knew	
foot		lady	
football		lamp	
formal		language	
four		last	
friend		learn (to), learned	
from		like (to), liked	
full		list	
girl		live (to), lived	
girls		look (to), looked	
give (to), gave		look for (to), looked for	
glass		man	
glasses		mango	
go (to), went		many	
good		match	
good bye		men	
grammar		middle	

Student Workbook

GLOSSARY

ENGLISH	NOTES	ENGLISH	NOTES
mistake		past	
mountain		pasta	
Mr. / Mrs. / Ms.		peace	
my		peaceful	
name		pen	
nationality		pencil	
nearby		people	
necklace		phone	
need (to), needed		phrase	
negative		picture	
neighbor		pizza	
new		place	
next		plan (to), planned	
nice		plane (airplane)	
night		play (to), played	
no		please (to), pleased	
nobody		plural	
noon		pocket	
not		policeman	
notebook		possessive	
noun		post (to), posted	
now		practice (to), practiced	
number		preposition	
nurse		progressive	
o'clock		pronoun	
often		put (to), put	
on		quarter	
on the left		radio	
on the right		rain (to), rained	
on the way		read (to), read	
one (pronoun)		ready	
opposite		receptionist	
ordinal		red	
other		regular	
our		reservation	
outline		reserve (to), reserved	
outside		restaurant	
page		return (to), returned	
paint (to), painted		ride (to), rode	
pair of gloves		ring	
pair of shoes		road	
paper		robe	
park		roller-blades	
partner		room	
party		say (to), said	

Student Workbook

GLOSSARY

ENGLISH	NOTES	ENGLISH	NOTES
see (to), saw		tie	
sentence		time	
sew (to), sewed		today	
shoe		too	
short		town	
show (to), showed		toy	
sick		tree	
singular		T-shirt	
sister		umbrella	
sit (to), sat		under	
six		usually	
skis		verb	
sleep (to), slept		very	
small		waiter	
snow		waitress	
snowshoes		walk (to), walked	
soccer		wallet	
some		want (to), wanted	
someone		watch	
something		wear (to), wore	
sometimes		week	
son		well	
so-so		what	
speak (to), spoke		where	
specific		who	
Sprite		whose	
stand (to), stood		wife	
stone		window	
student		with	
study (to), studied		woman	
surname		women	
table		work	
talk about (to), talked about		write (to), wrote	
tea		your	
teacher		yours	
teacup			
thank you			
theater			
their			
there are			
there is			
things			
third			
thirsty			
this			

Student Workbook

BEGINNERS ESL LESSON PLANS BOOK 2

TEACHER'S GUIDE

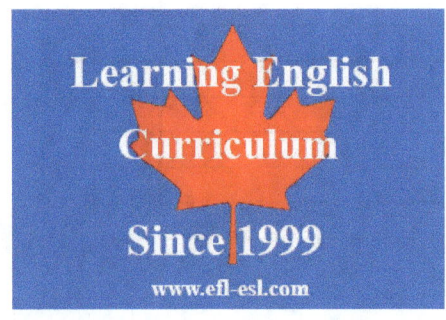

Student Workbook

Student Workbook

TEACHING PHILOSOPHY

Our philosophy means that the students and teachers can combine fun and learning, while communicating in English. This is a structured approach, meaning that each new concept is mastered in a conversational English environment before another is introduced. During the past decade, research has shown that the students learn more effectively if the teaching of grammar is integrated with a communicative approach to the learning of the English language.

This program is written for students 13 years and older. We introduce the basic tenses and other structures in a logical sequence, integrating them with light hearted activities that provide practice in a conversational setting. The combination achieved in Learning English Curriculum has proved to be popular with the students and successful in achieving its goals.

TIMING AND LESSON STRUCTURE

The most successful order of presentation for the lessons is outlined below:
- Greeting the students in English
- Oral questions (20 to 30 minutes)

Oral Questions may be done before or after the new lesson has been introduced.
The order suggested in the Student's Book should be adapted to the needs of the group.
- Introduction of a new lesson or continuation of a past lesson.
- Completion of exercises and / or partner activities
- Ending with a more relaxed conversational activity

VOCABULARY

The new words introduced in each lesson are listed under the title and may be introduced in any of the following ways:
- The teacher may write the words on the blackboard and use them in sentences.
- The teacher can dramatize, draw or use the pictures to explain the words.
- The students can work in small groups with their dictionaries.

ORAL QUESTIONS

The oral questions are designed to provide practice in speaking.
The questions and answers stress grammatical structure, and word order of the English language.
When our students completed surveys where Oral Questions were rated "helpful / not helpful" on a scale of 1 to 10, **Oral Questions were consistently rated as "10 - very helpful".**
Teaching this Conversational English program without using the oral questions will result in the lessons becoming too difficult for the students.

These questions provide the basic models of the English Language.
They are a vital part of the program, giving practice, review and an opportunity for the teacher to expand the language to talk about local events.

Student Workbook

SUGGESTIONS FOR PRESENTING ORAL QUESTIONS
If the group has fewer than 15 students the teacher can work with the whole group.

- It is best to begin at the start of the oral question and work down, as the first questions can be a review.
- Avoid asking students in the order in which they sit. Their attention will be the best if they don't know who you are going to ask next!
- It is important to write difficult questions on the blackboard and discuss the possible answers with the students.
- Always be willing to use the blackboard to clarify a question or answer. Encourage the students to request such clarification.
- Be sure to ask the same question a number of times until the students can answer fluently. This is especially important for the difficult questions.
- As the basic questions and answers are learned, it will be important for the teacher to adapt and expand the questions and answers. The given questions and suggested answers provide basic grammatically correct English. It will be helpful if teachers try to provide additional humorous and / or questions about local events.

ALTERNATIVE WAYS OF PRESENTING THE ORAL QUESTIONS SO THEY CAN BE ADAPTED TO DIFFERENT GROUPS

If the whole group approach is not appropriate to the situation then the presentation of the questions may be adapted in the following ways:

The class can be divided in half.
One copy of the oral questions can be given to each pair of students in one half of the class.
They can then take turns asking each other the questions. Meanwhile the teacher can be working orally with the other half as explained above.
Working with half of the class at a time is well suited to using volunteers.

EXERCISES
The exercises are designed to give the students practice in important points of grammar.
These can be done in class or assigned as homework. Due to the differences between the English language and other languages, students should understand the meaning of each sentence, but they should avoid making a direct translation, (a translation of each word). Word by word translation often changes the meaning, takes too much time, and prevents the student from learning the correct English word order. Teachers should use their discretion when deciding the order in which the students complete the exercises.

ACTIVITIES
The activities are often designed to take place in a more relaxed atmosphere, with the students moving around the room, and practicing what they have learned. The goal of these activities is for the students to gain practice, and not to finish the activity quickly. They will require supervision, so that they do practice the English, and not complete the activity in their own language. If time is limited, then an activity may be skipped and returned to at a later time. Teachers should use their discretion when deciding the order in which the students complete the activities.

SEATING ARRANGEMENT
We suggest that the students sit facing each other. A U shaped configuration works well.

Student Workbook

TESTS

The tests are a part of the learning process. They allow the students to identify the areas they need to study. When marking the sentence answers, subtract one mark for each error.
- If a student has one mistake, he or she will get 3 marks for that answer
- If a student has two mistakes, he or she will get 2 marks for that answer
- If a student has three mistakes, he or she will get 1 mark for that answer
- If a student has four or more mistakes, he or she won't get any marks

GIVE SPECIAL ATTENTION TO INDIVIDUAL NEEDS WHEN MARKING

The teacher should use discretion when marking. Some students work very hard but have difficulty. They should be given the best possible mark. Some students learn easily but become careless, so they should be marked down for their mistakes. In other words, the teacher needs to be aware of the needs of the students. The tests are designed to make most of the students feel good about their English but also give a clear signal to those who aren't making satisfactory progress.

WHAT KIND OF MISTAKES SHOULD BE CONSIDERED?

Marks should be deducted for:
- not knowing the right vocabulary
- word order mistakes
- grammatical errors
- no marks are given if the student doesn't understand the question

Do **not** deduct marks for spelling mistakes if you can understand what the student means.
Students with marks above 80% are ready to continue with the program.
Test answers are included in the Guide.

ANSWERS TO THE ORAL TEST QUESTIONS

The teachers have the choice of having the students answer orally or in writing. As some of the teachers are speaking English as a second language, it might be difficult for them to test pronunciation. If the teacher can understand what the student is saying then the pronunciation should be accepted. Internationally, it is acceptable if the speaker is understood.

The tests are out of 50 except for the last test in Part 1 and in Part 2.
There are no absolutes when assessing test marks. Many factors always enter into the mark. These can range from the student being sick that day to some problem at home. It's also possible that the student missed a lot of classes due to illness.

The purpose of these tests is to allow the students to see where they are having difficulty. This lets them know where they should spend their time when they study.
This is the most important aspect of the tests.

ANSWERS

Answers in the Guide are written in italics. The suggested answers are the most likely, but others are possible.

GLOSSARY

The glossary contains the vocabulary for this book.
The verbs are shown in the infinitive form: do (to).
The past tenses are included for reference in the glossary, shown as: infinitive, past tense.

Student Workbook

Lesson 21

NOTE: In North America, we go to the theater for plays, or for films, which are called "movies". In England, movies are seen in a cinema, and plays in a theater.

ORAL QUESTIONS

Who is across from you?	_____ is across from me.
Who is in (at) the corner of the room? _____	_____ is in (at) the corner of the room.
Do you go along the street sometimes?	Yes, I go along the street sometimes.

The students are to look at the map on Page 38 of their Student Book.

Where do the Carters live?	The Carters live <u>at</u> 11 Kent Street.
What street do they live on?	They live <u>on</u> Kent Street.
Where is the restaurant?	It's <u>at</u> 34 Main Street.
	It's <u>on</u> Main Street.
Where is the church?	It's <u>at</u> 22 Pine Street.
	It's <u>on</u> Pine Street.
Where is the park?	It's <u>on</u> Park Street.
Where is the school?	It's <u>at</u> the corner of Wilson St. and Main St.
	It's <u>at</u> 86 Main St.
Where is the supermarket?	It is <u>on</u> West St.
How does Raymond go to school?	He walks to school.
How do you go from the restaurant to the church?	You walk across Main St. to Park St. and along Park St. to Pine St.
How do you go from the school to the park?	Walk along Main Street to Park Street.
How many blocks is it from Main to Kent St.?	It's two blocks.
How many people do you see in the school?	There are about eleven people.
Do you have some horses?	Yes, I have some horses.
	No, I don't have any horses.
Do you have some sons?	Yes, I have some sons.
	No, I don't have any sons.
Do you have some daughters?	Yes, I have some daughters.
	No, I don't have any daughters.
Do you have some hamburgers?	Yes, I have some hamburgers.
	No, I don't have any hamburgers.
Do you have some matches?	Yes, I have some matches.
	No, I don't have any matches.
Do you have some pens?	Yes, I have some pens.
	No, I don't have any pens

Teachers Guide

Lesson 21 Continued

PAGE 43   ANSWERS TO THE WORKBOOK QUESTIONS: **EXERCISE 1**

1. How do Ruth and Raymond get to school?
   Ruth and Raymond walk to school.
2. Where is the school?
   The school is at the corner of Main and Wilson Streets.
   The school is at 86 Main Street.
3. What is across from the park?
   The restaurant is across from the park.
4. Where is the supermarket?
   The supermarket is on West Street.

PAGE 43   ANSWERS TO THE WORKBOOK QUESTIONS   **ACTIVITY 3**

1. Do you have some cats? (no)   *No, I don't have any cats.*
2. Do you see some hands? (yes)   *Yes, I see some hands.*
3. Do you see some dishes? (no)   *No, I don't see any dishes.*
4. Do you have some apples? (no)   *No, I don't have any apples.*
5. Do you see a church? (no)   *No, I don't see a church.*
6. Do you see some flowers? (yes)   *Yes, I see some flowers.*
7. Do you have some matches? (no)   *No, I don't have any matches.*
8. Do you have some books? (yes)   *Yes, I have some books.*

PAGE 44   ANSWERS TO THE WORKBOOK QUESTIONS: **EXERCISE 2**

Answer the following questions in the positive and negative:

1. How many pens do you have?
   (Positive) *I have _____ pens.*
   (Negative) *I don't have any pens.*
2. How many dogs do you have?
   (Positive) *I have one dog.*
   (Negative) *I don't have any dogs.*

PAGE 44   ANSWERS TO THE WORKBOOK QUESTIONS   **EXERCISE 3**

1. Who is sitting across from you?   _____ *is sitting across from me.*
2. Who is on your right?   _____ *is on my right.*
3. Do you sometimes walk along the street?   *Yes, I sometimes walk along the street.*
4. Who is on your left?   _____ *is on my left.*
5. Do you get apples at the supermarket?   *Yes, I get apples at the supermarket.*
   No, I don't get any apples at the...
6. Do you live across from a church?   *Yes, I live across from a church.*
   No, I don't live across from a church.
7. Is there a park in your town?   *Yes, there is a park in our / my town.*
8. Do you go to the theatre?   *Yes, I go to the theater.*
   No, I don't go to the theater.
9. Is the school across from the Carter's house?   *No, the school is not across from the Carter's house.*

PAGE 45   ANSWERS TO THE BINGO   **ACTIVITY 4**

2 my (mine)	14 theater	9 our (ours)	4 supermarket	18 Canadian
23 outside	19 his	17 house	13 hat	5 behind
6 here	7 boy	10 to come	24 grandfather	16 good
15 chair	22 dictionary	**1 corner**	20 Vancouver	8 left
3 to like	11 restaurant	21 can't	12 don't	

Teachers Guide

Lesson 22

To the teacher: This logo means to memorize the phrases.
Phrases beside this logo have irregular grammatical patterns. Use them often.

ORAL QUESTIONS

Do you eat hamburgers on your way home from school?	Yes, I eat hamburgers on my way home... No, I don't eat hamburgers on my way...
What days do you come to English classes?	I come to English classes on _____.
Do you eat dinner at home?	Yes, I eat dinner at home. No, I don't eat dinner at home.
Does your sister eat dinner at home?	Yes, she eats dinner at home. No, she doesn't eat dinner at home. I don't have a sister.
Do you go to town on Saturdays?	Yes, I go to town on Saturdays. No, I don't go to town on Saturdays.
Do you usually volunteer?	Yes, I usually volunteer. No, I don't usually volunteer.
Do you like to sew?	Yes, I (sometimes) like to sew. No, I don't like to sew.
Do you enjoy English classes?	Yes, I enjoy English classes. No, I don't enjoy English classes.
Does he/she enjoy English classes?	Yes, he/she enjoys English classes. No, he/she doesn't enjoy English classes.
Do you go home after class?	Yes, I go home after class. No, I don't go home after class.
Do you enjoy sports?	Yes, I enjoy sports. No, I don't enjoy sports.
Do you go hiking?	Yes, I go hiking. No, I don't go hiking.
Do you buy hamburgers after class?	Yes, I buy hamburgers after class. No, I don't buy hamburgers after class.
Do you buy apples on Fridays?	Yes, I buy apples on Fridays. No, I don't buy apples on Fridays.
Do you usually eat at home?	Yes, I usually eat at home. No, I don't usually eat at home.
Do you have a table / desk?	Yes, I have a table/desk. No, I don't have a table/desk.
Where do you eat lunch / dinner?	I eat lunch / dinner at _____.
Does your town have some restaurants?	Yes, my town has some restaurants.
What days do you come to class?	I come to class on _____.
What days are you at home?	I am at home on _____.

Teachers Guide

Lesson 22 Continued

PAGE 41 ANSWERS TO THE STUDENT READER QUESTIONS: ACTIVITY 4:

1. I like to _____.
2. I go to school on _____.
3. I usually eat supper at home.
4. Yes, I like to hike.
   No, I don't like to hike.
5. Yes, I like hamburgers.
   No, I don't like hamburgers.
6. I like sewing.
   I don't like sewing.
7. I do interesting things on _____.
8. Yes, I eat something on the way home.
   No, I don't eat on the way home.
9. Yes, I (sometimes) do volunteer work.
   No, I don't do volunteer work.
10. I like to eat _____.

PAGE 46 ANSWERS TO THE WORKBOOK QUESTIONS: **EXERCISE 1**

1. When do Raymond's parents go to church? They go to church on Sundays.
2. What does Ruth like to do? Ruth likes to sew.
3. Who works as a volunteer with Ruth? Nancy works as a volunteer with Ruth.
4. When do they volunteer at the hospital? They volunteer on Saturdays and Sundays.
5. What do they sometimes buy on the way home? They sometimes buy something to eat.
6. What do Raymond and his friend do? They go hiking.
7. When do they hike? They hike after school on Mondays and Wednesdays.
8. What volunteer work do they do? They volunteer as guides for tourists.
9. What do they often buy on the way home? They often buy hamburgers on the way home.
   Yes, I work as a volunteer.
10. Do you do volunteer work?
    No, I don't work as a volunteer.

PAGES 46 & 47 ANSWERS TO THE WORKBOOK QUESTIONS: **EXERCISES 2 & 3**

Put these sentences into the singular. Put the following sentences into the plural.

1. He / She has a neighbor   1. They are students..
2. There is a friend here.   2. We have dogs.
3. There is a store.   3. They have glasses
4. The street has a dog.   4. They are from Australia.
5. There is one (a) church.   5. There are mountains beside the cities.
6. The city has one (a) restaurant. 6. They meet friends.

PAGE 47 ANSWERS TO THE WORKBOOK QUESTIONS: **EXERCISE 4**

Raymond Carter is *an* Australian. He lives with his family *at* 11 Kent Street. His sister is Ruth. She lives *at* home with her family *on* Kent Street. Raymond's neighbor is Ming. His mother and father are *from* China, but they are Australians now. Ming lives *at* 13 Kent Street. Raymond and Ming are friends.

Nancy is Ming's neighbor. She is Ruth's friend, too. Nancy lives *at* 15 Kent Street. She lives in an apartment *on* the third floor. Ming, Nancy, Raymond and Ruth are neighbors. They all live *on* Kent Street.

Teachers Guide

Lesson 23

To the teacher:

"Can" has more than one meaning. It can be used to give <u>permission</u>.
EXAMPLE: The mother said to her daughter, "You <u>can</u> stay out until 10:00 tonight."

It also means <u>to be able</u> to do something.
In the present tense, "can" is usually used instead of <u>to be able</u>.
EXAMPLE: He can hike up the mountain.

"To be able" is more commonly used in combination with other auxiliaries.
This lesson teaches the use of "<u>can</u>" - meaning to be able.

The present progressive tense:
This tense is used with the words "hiking" and "standing" in this lesson.
Explain that the tense will be taught later if the students ask.

ORAL QUESTIONS

Can you see me?	*Yes, I can see you.*
Do you hike on the mountains?	*Yes, I hike on the mountains.* *No, I don't hike on the mountains.*
Do you see your family at suppertime?	*Yes, I see my family at suppertime.* *No, I don't see my family at suppertime.*
Do you like the mountains?	*Yes, (Sure) I like the mountains.* *No, I don't like the mountains.*
Can you go to the mountains today?	*Yes, I can go to the mountains today.* *No, I can't go to the mountains today.*
Can you hike through deep snow?	*Yes, I can hike through deep snow.* *No, I can't hike through deep snow.*
Can you walk to English class?	*Yes, I can walk to English class.* *No, I can't walk to English class.*
Do you need to wear warm clothes today?	*Yes, I need to wear warm clothes today.* *No, I don't need to wear warm clothes today.*
Can you see through a window?	*Yes, I can see through a window.*
Does this pen belong to me?	*Yes, it belongs to you.* *No, it doesn't belong to you.*
Is this book his / hers?	*Yes, it's his / hers.* *No, it isn't his / hers.*
Can you speak English now?	*Yes, I can speak English now.*
Can you fly to English class?	*Yes, I can fly to English class.* *No, I can't fly to English class.*
Is there some deep snow at the top of the mountain?	*Yes, there is some deep snow at the top of the mountain.*

Teachers Guide

Lesson 23 Continued

PAGE 48 ANSWERS TO THE WORKBOOK QUESTIONS EXERCISE 1
EXERCISE 1 Answer the questions in sentences.

1. What do Sarah and Peter do? — They hike on the mountain (near their home).
2. Is the snow cold? — Yes, the snow is cold.
3. Is it colder at the top of the mountain? — Yes, it's colder at the top of the mountain.
4. What do they want to do? — They want to hike (head) to the top.
5. Do they have warm clothes? — Yes, they have warm clothes.
6. Do they decide to hike to the top? — Yes, they decide to hike to the top.
7. Do you hike on the mountains? — Yes, I hike on the mountain.
   No, I don't hike on the mountain.
8. Can you see the other side of a mountain from your home? — No, I can't see the other side of the mountain from my home.

   I can see other mountains.
9. Do you wear warm clothes when it's cold? — Yes, I wear warm clothes when it's cold.

PAGE 48 ANSWERS TO THE WORKBOOK QUESTIONS EXERCISE 2

clothes	you wear them
snow	it's very cold
sure	yes
cannot	can't
to head	to go
warm	not too hot or too cold
trail	a small road
supper	you eat it

PAGE 49 ANSWERS TO THE WORKBOOK QUESTIONS EXERCISE 3

1. I'm in English class. / I'm at home. / I'm at school.
2. I live at _____ _____.
3. The windows are on the left / right.
   The windows are on my left / right.
   The windows are behind me.

4. The door is on the right / left.
   The door is in front of me.
   The door is behind me.

5. There are _____ students in the classroom.
6. You walk along Main St. to Park Street and then along Park St. to Pine St.

7. The stores are on West St.
8. It's hers.
9. It's mine.
10. It's theirs.
11. They're ours.
12. They're his.

Teacher Guide

Lesson 23 Continued

PAGE 50   ANSWERS TO THE WORKBOOK QUESTIONS ACTIVITY 3:
1. *No, the dog is not on the table.*
2. *The book is on the table.*
3. *The dog is between the lamp and the table.*
4. *No, the lamp isn't beside the table.*
5. *Yes, the dog is beside the table.*
6. *No, the dog is not under the table.*
7. *No, there is one book on the table.*
8. *The dog is between the lamp and the table.*
9. *No, the book is on the table.*
10. *Yes, I have a dog under my desk.*
    No, I don't have a dog under my desk.

ACTIVITY 4

Photocopy and cut the items from Page 92 of this guide into separate cards. Divide the class into Team 1 and Team 2. Give out the cards so that each student has one or more, and they are equally divided between the teams.

The first student on Team 1 is to ask a student on Team 2 their question. If the student answers correctly, they get 1 point for their team. Then Team 2 asks a student on Team 1. Continue until all the questions have been asked.

Each student should ask and answer at least one question.

Lesson 23 Continued

ACTIVITY 4 CONTINUED:

Can you drive a car?
Yes, I can drive a car.
No, I can't drive a car.

Can you hike through deep snow?
Yes, I can hike through deep snow.
No, I can't hike through deep snow.

Do you want to learn English?
Yes, I want to learn English.
No, I don't want to learn English.

Do you try to answer English questions?
Yes, I try to answer English questions.

Do you wear warm clothes when it's cold?
Yes, I wear warm clothes when it's cold.
No, I don't wear warm clothes when it's cold.

Do you go to the stores in town?
Yes, I go to the stores in town.
No, I don't go to the stores in town.

Do you go to the temple?
Yes, I go to the temple.
No, I don't go to the temple.

Is the theater across from your home?
Yes, the theater is across from my home.
No, the theater isn't across from my home.

Do you know some English words?
Yes, I know some English words.

Do you hike in the mountains?
Yes, I hike in the mountains.
No, I don't hike in the mountains.

Do you have warm clothes?
Yes, I have warm clothes.
No, I don't have warm clothes.

Can you see the mountains from your home?
Yes, I can see the mountains from my home.
No, I can't see the mountains from my home.

Do you try to hike through deep snow?
Yes, I try to hike through deep snow.
No, I don't try to hike through deep snow.

Do you like to walk along mountain trails?
Yes, I like to walk along mountain trails.
No, I don't like to walk along mountain trails.

Do you like to use a sewing machine?
Yes, I like to use a sewing machine.
No, I don't like to use a sewing machine.

Do you do volunteer work?
Yes, I do volunteer work.
No, I don't do volunteer work.

Do you eat lunch in a restaurant?
Yes, I eat lunch in a restaurant.
No, I don't eat lunch in a restaurant.

Do you see some people on the way home?
Yes, I see some people on the (my) way home.
No, I don't see any people on the (my) way home.

Teacher Guide

Lesson 24

Review the Oral Questions for Lessons 21 to 24 as needed.

| PAGE 51 | ANSWERS TO THE WORKBOOK QUESTIONS | | | | EXERCISE 1 |

neighbors	*you live beside them*	**floor**	*your desk is on it*	**sure**	*yes*
home	*where you live*	**a chair**	*you sit on it*	**great**	*very good*
a friend	*someone you like*	**movie**	*you see it in a theatre*	**lunch**	*you eat it at 12:00*
dictionary	*it has words in it*	**to stretch**	*to extend from place to place*		

PAGE 51   ANSWERS TO THE WORKBOOK QUESTIONS   EXERCISE 2

1. Do you have a cat under your table?   *No, I don't have a cat under my table.*
2. Where does your neighbor live?   *My neighbor lives at (number) on (no number)*
   My neighbor lives beside me.
3. What is outside your window?   *A _____ is outside my window.*
   There is a tree outside my window.
4. Do you drink water?   *Yes, I drink water.*
5. What is in your hand?   *A ____ is in my hand. Some ____ are in my hand.*
6. Are you at your home now?   *No, I'm not at home now.*
7. Do you live on the fifteenth floor?   *Yes, I live on the fifteenth floor.*
   No, I don't live on the fifteenth floor.
8. Do you hike in the mountains?   *Yes, I hike in the mountains. / No, I don't hike…*
9. How many students are here?   *There are _____ students here. / ____ students are here.*
10. Do you volunteer on Sundays?   *Yes, I volunteer on Sundays.*
    No, I don't volunteer on Sundays.

PAGE 52   ANSWERS TO THE WORKBOOK QUESTIONS   ACTIVITY 3

1. *Yes, he/ she has some dogs.*
   No, he / she doesn't have any dogs.
2. *Yes, she has some lamps.*
   No, she doesn't have any lamps.
3. *Yes, he / she goes to the theater in the city.*
   No, he / she doesn't go to the theater in the city.
4. *Yes, _____ has a dictionary.*
   No, _____ doesn't have a dictionary.
5. *The teacher is _____.*
6. *Yes, my friend has some cats.*
   No, my friend doesn't have any cats.
7. *Yes, my friend has a book/some books.*
8. *Yes, my friend has some pencils.*
   No, my friend doesn't have any pencils.
9. *Yes, he/she has a sister. / No, he/she doesn't have a sister.*
10. *Yes, he/she buys some food in the supermarket.*
11. *Yes, he/she can run.*
12. *No, he/she can't fly.*

Lesson 24 Continued

PAGE 52 **ANSWERS TO THE WORKBOOK QUESTIONS** **EXERCISE 3**

Sarah and Peter **_hike_** through the snow. As they go up the **_mountain_** the snow gets deeper. It is **_cold_** up there but they have **_warm_** clothes. When they look down, they can see their **_town_** below. It looks very **_small_** from up there. The snow is **_deep_** at the top of the mountain. They can see the **_beautiful_** mountains that stretch on and on. They decide to enjoy them and have something to **_eat_**.

PAGE 53 **ANSWERS TO THE WORKBOOK QUESTIONS** **EXERCISE 4**

1. Where are Sarah and Peter? — They are on the mountain.
2. Can they see the town below? — Yes, they can see the town below.
3. How does the town look? — The town looks small.
4. Can they see the building where they live? — Yes, they can see it.
5. Where is their building? — It's on the right.
6. What is the snow like at the top of the mountain? — It's very deep.
7. Do they get to the top of the mountain? — Yes, they get to the top of the mountain.
8. What do they see on the other side of the mountain? — They see beautiful snowy mountains.
9. Do you live beside a mountain? — Yes, I live beside a mountain. / No, I don't live beside a mountain.
10. Who has a good idea? — Sarah has a good idea.
11. What is her good idea? — Her good idea is to enjoy the mountains and have something to eat.

TEST 6 TOTAL MARKS: 50
ANSWERS FOR TEST 6
(Questions 1-9, 4 marks each)

1. The theater is at 69 Main Street/ the corner of Main and Mason St.
2. Bob's house is across from the Park.
   The supermarket is across from the Park.
3. Bob's house is between the Park and Pat's restaurant.
4. Yes, I hike up the mountain. / No, I don't hike up the mountain.
5. No, I don't have a cat under my desk.
6. Yes, there is some juice on the teacher's desk.
   No, there isn't any juice on the teacher's desk.
7. Yes, I have some matches.
   No, I don't have any matches.
8. No, dogs can't fly.
9. I come to English classes on _____.

NOTE: Don't subtract marks for the days of the week spelling mistakes if you can understand the word.
The days of the week: (2 marks each)

10. Sunday 11. Monday 12. Tuesday 13. Wednesday 14. Thursday 15. Friday 16. Saturday

Teacher Guide

TEST 6   NAME_____

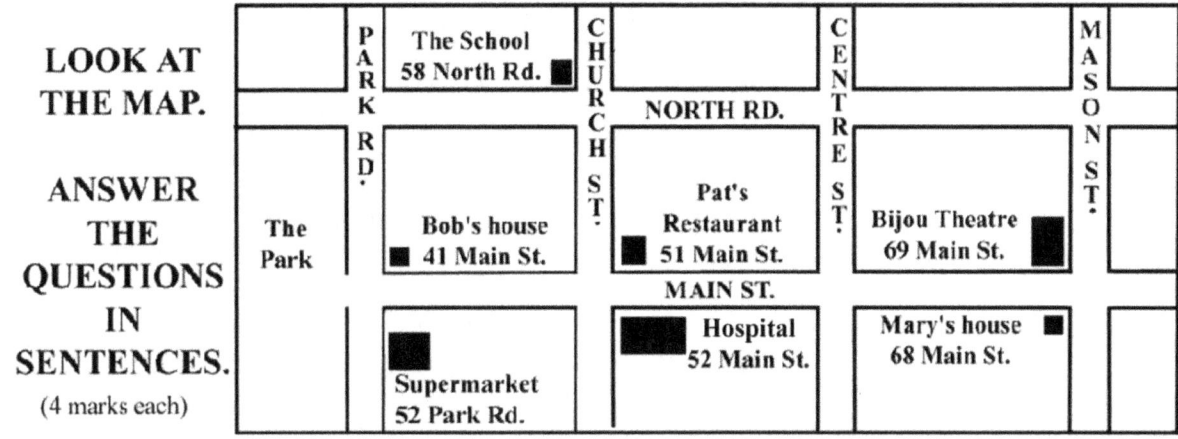

LOOK AT THE MAP.

ANSWER THE QUESTIONS IN SENTENCES.
(4 marks each)

1. Where is the theater?
   _____

2. What is across from the Park?
   _____

3. What is between the Park and Pat's Restaurant?
   _____

4. Do you hike up the mountain?
   _____

5. Do you have a cat under your desk?
   _____

6. Is there some juice on the teacher's desk?
   _____

7. Do you have some matches?
   _____

8. Can dogs fly?
   _____

9. What days do you come to English classes?
   _____

What are the days of the week? (2 marks each)

10. _____   11. _____   12. _____   13. _____

14. _____   15. _____   16. _____

Teacher Guide

Lesson 25

ORAL QUESTIONS

Did you live here last year?   Yes, I lived here last year.
No, I didn't live here last year.

Did you play basketball yesterday?   Yes, I played basketball yesterday.
No, I didn't play basketball yesterday.

Did you walk to class today?   Yes, I walked to class today.
No, I didn't walk to class today.

Did you like the theater last night?   Yes, I liked the theater last night.
No, I didn't like the theater last night.

Did you hike up the mountain today?   Yes, I hiked up the mountain today.
No, I didn't hike up the mountain today.

Did you enjoy some hamburgers last week?   Yes, I enjoyed some hamburgers last week.
No, I didn't enjoy any hamburgers last week.

Did you live in Vietnam last year?   Yes, I lived in Vietnam last year.
No, I didn't live in Vietnam last year.

Did you walk home from class yesterday?   Yes, I walked home from class yesterday.
No, I didn't walk home from class yesterday.

Did you play on a basketball team last year?   Yes, I played on a basketball team last year.
No, I didn't play on a basketball team last year.

Did your cat follow you this morning?   Yes, my cat followed me this morning.
No, my cat didn't follow me this morning.

Did you phone your friend last night?   Yes, I phoned my friend last night.
No, I didn't phone my friend last night.

Did you ask your friend to dinner yesterday?   Yes, I asked my friend to dinner yesterday.
No, I didn't ask my friend to dinner yesterday.

Did you watch television last night?   Yes, I watched television last night.
No, I didn't watch television last night.

Did your soccer team play last week?   Yes, my soccer team played last week.
No, my soccer team didn't play last week.
I don't play on a soccer team.

Did you close the classroom door today?   Yes, I closed the classroom door today.
No, I didn't close the classroom door today.

Did you answer the telephone this morning?   Yes, I answered the telephone this morning.
No, I didn't answer the telephone this morning.

Did your friend phone you last night?   Yes, he/she phoned me last night.
No, he/she didn't phone me last night.

Did you study English last night?   Yes, I studied English last night.
No, I didn't study English last night.

Teacher Guide

Lesson 25 Continued

ACTIVITY 5: Photocopy and cut the items below into separate cards. Divide the class into Team 1 and Team 2. Give out the cards so that each student has one or more, and they are equally divided between the teams. The first student on Team 1 is to ask a student on Team 2 their question. If the student answers correctly, he / she gets 1 point for their team. Then Team 2 asks a student on Team 1. Continue until all the questions have been asked.

Each student should ask and answer at least one question.

Did your dog follow you to class?
Yes, my dog followed me to class.
No, my dog didn't follow me to class.

Did you do volunteer work today?
Yes, I did volunteer work today.
No, I didn't do volunteer work today.

Did you enjoy the theater last night?
Yes, I enjoyed the theater last night.
No, I didn't enjoy the theater last night.

Did you phone your friend last Saturday?
Yes, I phoned my friend last Saturday.
No, I didn't phone my friend last Saturday.

Did you enjoy English class yesterday?
Yes, I enjoyed English class yesterday.
No, I didn't enjoy English class yesterday.

Did you walk to the park last Tuesday?
Yes, I walked to the park last Tuesday.
No, I didn't walk to the park last Tuesday.

Did you walk to the movies last Saturday?
Yes, I walked to the movies last Saturday.
No, I didn't walk to the movies last Saturday.

Did you phone your neighbor last Monday?
Yes, I phoned my neighbor last Monday.
No, I didn't phone my neighbor last Monday.

Did you live in the United States last year?
Yes, I lived in the United States last year.
No, I didn't live in the United States last year.

Did you watch television last week?
Yes, I watched television last week.
No, I didn't watch television last week.

Did you play basketball last week?
Yes, I played basketball last week.
No, I did not play basketball last week.

Did you hike up a mountain last Friday?
Yes, I hiked up a mountain last Friday.
No, I did not hike up a mountain last Friday.

Did you answer a question in class today?
Yes, I answered a question in class today.
No, I didn't answer a question in class today.

Did you phone a restaurant last Wednesday?
Yes, I phoned a restaurant last Wednesday.
No, I didn't phone a restaurant last Wednesday.

Did your friend like the theater last Saturday?
Yes, my friend liked the theater last Saturday.
No, my friend didn't like the theater last Saturday.

Did you live in an apartment last year?
Yes, I lived in an apartment last year.
No, I didn't live in an apartment last year.

Teacher Guide

Lesson 25 Continued

PAGE 54 — ANSWERS TO THE WORKBOOK QUESTIONS — **EXERCISE 1**

to need	*needed*
to watch	*watched*
to phone	*phoned*
to play	*played*
to close	*closed*
to follow	*followed*
to look	*looked*
to decide	*decided*
to correct	*corrected*

PAGE 54 — ANSWERS TO THE WORKBOOK QUESTIONS — **EXERCISE 2**

did   didn't

PAGE 54 — ANSWERS TO THE WORKBOOK QUESTIONS — **EXERCISE 3**

1. Did you play basketball last night? — *Yes, I played basketball last night.*
2. Did you watch television last night? — *Yes, I watched television last night.*
3. Did you live in India last year? — *Yes, I lived in India last year.*
4. Did your friends play basketball yesterday? — *Yes, my friends played basketball yesterday.*
5. Did you like the theater last night? — *Yes, I liked the theater last night.*
6. Did you walk to class today? — *Yes, I walked to class today.*
7. Did you hike up the mountain yesterday? — *Yes, I hiked up the mountain yesterday.*

PAGE 55 — ANSWERS TO THE WORKBOOK QUESTIONS — **EXERCISE 4**

1. *I phoned my friend.*
2. *She closed the door.*
3. *They liked the watch.*
4. *He lived in Russia.*
5. *They asked to play basketball.*
6. *The dogs followed her.*
7. *We enjoyed the afternoon.*
8. *He answered the phone.*

PAGE 55 — ANSWERS TO THE WORKBOOK QUESTIONS — **EXERCISE 5**

to watch	*to look for a long time*	to stretch	*to extend*
to do	*did*	food	*what you eat*
year	*365 days*	small	*not big*
weekend	*Saturday and Sunday*	machine	*you make it work for you*
to follow	*to go behind something*		

PAGE 46 — ANSWERS TO THE STUDENT READER QUESTIONS — **ACTIVITY 4**

They talked on the phone.   *They played soccer.*
They watched television.   *They hiked through the snow.*

Teacher Guide

Lesson 26

ORAL QUESTIONS

Did you eat something today?	Yes, I ate something today.
	No, I didn't eat anything today.
Did you come to class last week?	Yes, I came to class last week.
	No, I didn't come to class last week.
Did you go to school / work yesterday?	Yes, I went to _____ yesterday.
	No, I didn't go to _____ yesterday.
Did you meet your friend this morning?	Yes, I met my friend this morning.
	No, I didn't meet my friend this morning.
Did you buy a hamburger yesterday?	Yes, I bought a hamburger yesterday.
	No, I didn't buy a hamburger yesterday.
Did you hike up the mountain last week?	Yes, I hiked up the mountain last week.
	No, I didn't hike up the mountain last week.
Did you want to listen to a song?	Yes, I wanted to listen to a song.
	No, I didn't want to listen to a song.
Did you find your friend?	Yes, I found my friend.
	No, I didn't find my friend.
Did you buy an apple yesterday?	Yes, I bought an apple yesterday.
	No, I didn't buy an apple yesterday.
Where did you put your book?	I put my book on the table.
Did you go to the movies?	Yes, I went to the movies.
	No, I didn't go to the movies.
Did you have a dog last year?	Yes, I had a dog last year.
	No, I didn't have a dog last year.
Did you see your friend?	Yes, I saw my friend.
	No, I didn't see my friend.
Did you read a book last week?	Yes, I read a book last week.
	No, I didn't read a book last week.
Did you enjoy a video last week?	Yes, I enjoyed a video last week.
	No, I didn't enjoy a video last week.
Did you eat some chicken yesterday?	Yes, I ate some chicken yesterday.
	No, I didn't eat any chicken yesterday.
Did you begin English this year?	Yes, I began English this year.
	No, I didn't begin English this year.
Did you walk to town last week?	Yes, I walked to town last week.
	No, I didn't walk to town last week.
Did you eat a hamburger on the way home?	Yes, I ate a hamburger on the way home.
	No, I didn't eat a hamburger on the way...
Did you write a letter yesterday?	Yes, I wrote a letter yesterday.
	No, I didn't write a letter yesterday.
How many apples did you eat last week?	I ate _____ apples last week.
	I didn't eat any apples last week.

Teacher Guide

Lesson 26 Continued

PAGE 56 — **ANSWERS TO THE WORKBOOK QUESTIONS** — **EXERCISE 1**

found – to find   met – to meet
saw – to see   bought – to buy

PAGE 56 — **ANSWERS TO THE WORKBOOK QUESTIONS** — **EXERCISE 2**

1. Where did Craig Carter go? — He went to the video store.
2. What did Jessica find in the library? — She found some books.
3. Where did Ruth see good CD's? — She saw them at / in the music store.
4. Where did Raymond meet his friends? — He met his friends outside the theater.
5. What did they sometimes buy for supper? — They bought some pizza.

PAGE 56 — **ANSWERS TO THE WORKBOOK QUESTIONS** — **ACTIVITY 3**

1. Did you come to class yesterday? *(come)* — Yes, he/she came to class yesterday.
   No, he/she didn't come to class yesterday.
2. Did you go to a restaurant yesterday? *(go)* — Yes, he/she went to a restaurant yesterday.
   No, he/she didn't go to a restaurant yesterday.
3. Did you meet your friend last night? *(meet)* — Yes, he/she met his/her friend last night.
   No, he/she didn't meet his/her friend last night.
4. Did you eat lunch today? *(eat)* — Yes, he/she ate lunch today.
   No, he/she didn't eat lunch today.
5. Did you buy a hat last week? *(buy)* — Yes, he/she bought a hat last week.
   No, he/she didn't buy a hat last week.
6. Did you write to your friend last night? *(write)* — Yes, he/she wrote to his/her friend last night.
   No, he/she didn't write to his/her friend. last night.
7. Did you find your watch? *(find)* — Yes, he/she found his/her watch.
   No. he/she didn't find his/her watch.

PAGE 57 — **ANSWERS TO THE WORKBOOK QUESTIONS** — **EXERCISE 3**

a ticket	you buy it for a movie or a bus
library	you get books there
a movie	you watch it
a song	you listen to it
road	cars drive on it
Saturday	a day of the week
afternoon	the time after lunch
the latest	the newest
to go	went
to have	had
to see	saw

Teacher Guide

Lesson 26 Continued

PAGE 57 ANSWERS TO THE WORKBOOK QUESTIONS **EXERCISE 4**

Last month the Carters **_did_** (to do) many things on Saturdays. Craig **_went_** (to go) to the video store. Jessica usually **_looked_** (to look) for good books in the library.

Ruth **_liked_** (to like) to find good CD's in the music store. She often **_listened_** (to listen) with her friend Nancy. They **_enjoyed_** (to enjoy) learning the latest songs.

On Saturday afternoon Raymond usually **_met_** (to meet) many of his friends outside the theater. Sometimes they **_bought_** (to buy) tickets to see the movie. After the movie they **_walked_** (to walk) along the road to buy pizza.

PAGE 58 ANSWERS TO THE BINGO **ACTIVITY 4**
LIST 2:   **BINGO**

23	wrote	2	sat	8	ate
1	where you buy something	7	you find books there	13	you eat it
19	where the stores are	3	you listen to it	9	you write it
14	began	20	bought	6	hiked
15	you can close it	21	you can eat there	4	where you live
12	studied	18	came	24	met
10	you eat it at 12:00	16	you enjoy music there	22	you sit on it
5	a person you like	11	you live beside them	17	found

Teacher Guide

Lesson 27

REVIEW THE ORAL QUESTIONS FOR LESSON 26.

ORAL QUESTIONS USING "TO BE"

Were you at home last night?	Yes, I was at home last night.
	No, I wasn't at home last night.
Were you in town yesterday?	Yes, I was in town yesterday.
	No, I wasn't in town yesterday.
Were you with your friends today?	Yes, I was with my friends today.
	No, I wasn't with my friends today.
Were you in a restaurant today?	Yes, I was in a restaurant today.
	No, I wasn't in a restaurant today.
Were you at the movies last night?	Yes, I was at the movies last night.
	No, I wasn't at the movies last night.
Was your friend at home yesterday?	Yes, my friend was at home yesterday.
	No, my friend wasn't at home yesterday.
Was your friend at school yesterday?	Yes, my friend was at school yesterday.
	No, my friend wasn't at school yesterday.

PAGE 47   ANSWERS TO THE STUDENT BOOK QUESTIONS   ACTIVITY 1

1. **Were you at home last night?**
   Yes, I was at home last night.
   No, I wasn't at home last night.

2. **Were you at the theatre last week?**
   Yes, I was at the theater last week.
   No, I wasn't at the theater last week.

3. **Was your dog outside last night?**
   Yes, my dog was outside last night.
   No, my dog wasn't outside last night.

4. **Was your door closed last night?**
   Yes, my door was closed last night.
   No, my door wasn't closed last night.

5. **Was your friend at a restaurant?**
   Yes, my friend was at a restaurant.
   No, my friend wasn't at a restaurant.

6. **Was your friend in class yesterday?**
   Yes, my friend was in class yesterday.
   No, my friend wasn't in class yesterday.

7. **Were you in town yesterday?**
   Yes, I was in town yesterday.
   No, I wasn't in town yesterday.

8. **Were your friends at a restaurant last Saturday?**
   Yes, they were at the restaurant last Saturday.
   No, they weren't at the restaurant last Saturday.

9. **Were you in the library this morning?**
   Yes, I was in the library this morning.
   No, I wasn't in the library this morning.

10. **Were you at the movies last week?**
    Yes, I was at the movies last week.
    No, I wasn't at the movies last week.

Teacher Guide

Lesson 27 Continued

PAGE 59 ANSWERS TO THE WORKBOOK QUESTIONS **EXERCISE 1**

1. Where were you last night?
   I was _____ last night.

2. Were you in town yesterday?
   Yes, I was in town yesterday.
   No, I wasn't in town yesterday.

3. Was your cat inside last night?
   Yes, I was in front of the school today.
   No, I wasn't in front of the school today.

4. Was your friend in town yesterday?
   Yes, my friend was in town yesterday.
   No, my friend wasn't in town yesterday.

5. Was your friend at home last week?
   Yes, my friend was at home last week.
   No, my friend wasn't at home last week.

6. Was your dog at home this morning?
   Yes, my dog was at home this morning.
   No, my dog wasn't at home this morning.

7. Were you in front of the school today?
   Yes, my cat was inside last night.
   No, my cat wasn't inside last night.

8. Were you in the supermarket yesterday?
   Yes, I was in the supermarket yesterday.
   No, I wasn't in the supermarket yesterday.

PAGE 60 ANSWERS TO THE WORKBOOK QUESTIONS **EXERCISE 2**

1. Where were you yesterday? — *I was in the city.*
2. Was it cold outside this morning? — *Yes, it was cold.*
3. Were you at **school** yesterday? — *Yes, I was at school. / No, I wasn't at school.*
4. Were you at the **church/temple/mosque** last night? — *Yes, I was at the church/temple/mosque.*
   No, I wasn't at the church/temple/mosque last night.
5. Were many people in the **supermarket** yesterday afternoon? — *Yes, many people were in the supermarket.*
   No, there weren't many people in...
6. Were you in a **restaurant** last night? — *Yes, I was in a restaurant.*
   No, I wasn't in a restaurant.
7. Were you hiking in the **mountains** last weekend. — *Yes, I was hiking in the mountains.*
   No, I wasn't hiking in the mountains.

WORKBOOK PAGE 59 GUIDE PAGES 103 AND 104 **ACTIVITY 2 DIRECTIONS**

NOTE: "swimming", "running" are gerunds. (The -ing verb form that is used as a noun.)
Tell the students that the meaning is the same and that they will study gerunds at a later time.

Give each student one Role Card that describes the way he or she was last year.
They are to move about the room asking two other students the questions
on the information sheet on Page 59 of their workbook.

ANDREW SKALA (last year)
Age –18
Hobby - hiking
Friends: Arlene and Cleo

BILL VERNON (last year)
Age 15
Hobby - basketball
Friends: Amelia and Hazel

LINDA WATTS (last year)
Age - 16
Hobby - volunteering
Friends: Harvey and Fred

MARGARET SELKIRK (last year)
Age - 16
Hobby - reading
Friends: Arnold and Keith

Teacher Guide

Lesson 27 Continued
ROLE CARDS CONTINUED

ALAN DUNNING (last year)
Age - 17
Hobby - writing
Friends: Lynn and Millie

ELIZABETH FRASER (last year)
Age - 17
Hobby - hiking
Friends: Edmond and Robin

SARAH BATES (last year)
Age - 19
Hobby - reading
Friends: Ormond and Lester

DANIEL BLACK (last year)
Age - 18
Hobby: soccer
Friends: Wilma and Janice

RICHARD PATTERSON (last year)
Age: 20
Hobby: basketball
Friends: Lydia and Betty

ROSE MADSON (last year)
Age: 19
Hobby: cooking
Friends: Hugo and Roland

ANNE DENMAN (last year)
Age: 22
Hobby: reading
Friends: Roger and Orson

MARY TODD (last year)
Age: 19
Hobby: music
Friends: Lillie and Jenny

DEBORAH THORPE (last year)
Age: 21
Hobby: cooking
Friends: Milton and Brent

HELEN STONE (last year)
Age: 17
Hobby: running
Friends: Ralph and Ogden

TOM O'REILLY (last year)
Age: 20
Hobby: hiking
Friends: Gail and Juliet

SUSAN ROY (last year)
Age: 18
Hobby: basketball
Friends: Drew and Jacob

Teacher Guide

Lesson 28 - Review

ORAL QUESTIONS Review the oral questions for Lessons 25, 26 and 27.

ACTIVITY 3: Photocopy and cut the items below into separate cards. Divide the class into Team 1 and Team 2. Give each student one card. The first student on Team 1 is to ask a student on Team 2 their question. If the student answers correctly, they get 1 point for their team. Then Team 2 asks a student on Team 1. Continue until all the questions have been asked.
Each student should ask and answer at least one question.

Were you at the movies last night?
Yes, I was at the movies last night.
No, I wasn't at the movies last night.

Did you go to town yesterday?
Yes, I went to town yesterday.
No, I didn't go to town yesterday.

Did you ask your friend to the movies?
Yes, I asked my friend to the movies.
No, I didn't ask my friend to the movies.

Did you go to town last week?
Yes, I went to town last week.
No, I didn't go to town last week.

Did you buy some pizza yesterday?
Yes, I bought some pizza yesterday.
No, I didn't buy any pizza yesterday.

Were you in a store yesterday?
Yes, I was in a store yesterday.
No, I wasn't in a store yesterday.

Did you buy a hamburger today?
Yes, I bought a hamburger today.
No, I didn't buy a hamburger today.

Did you read a book this week?
Yes, I read a book this week.
No, I didn't read a book this week.

Did you write a letter this morning?
Yes, I wrote a letter this morning.
No, I didn't write a letter this morning.

Did you watch television this afternoon?
Yes, I watched television this afternoon.
No, I didn't watch television this afternoon.

Was your friend at the theatre last night?
Yes, my friend was at the theater last night.
No, my friend wasn't at the theater last night.

Were your friends in English class last year?
Yes, my friends were in English class last year.
No, my friends weren't in English class last year.

Did you eat something at home last night?
Yes, I ate something at home last night.
No, I didn't eat anything at home last night.

Did you meet your friends at the library today?
Yes, I met my friends at the library today.
No, I didn't meet my friends at the library today.

Did you hike with your friend last year?
Yes, I hiked with my friend last year.
No, I didn't hike with my friend last year.

Did you study your English this week?
Yes, I studied my English this week.
No, I didn't study my English this week.

Teacher Guide

Lesson 28 Continued

PAGE 61 ANSWERS TO THE WORKBOOK QUESTIONS **EXERCISE 1**

The Carters live (1) **on** Kent Street (2) **at** number 11. Raymond and Ruth walk (3) **along** Wilson Street (4) **to** their school. They walk two blocks to school. To go to the stores, they walk (5) **along** Kent Street to West Street, they turn right and walk two blocks. The stores are (6) **on** the right.

PAGE 61 ANSWERS TO THE WORKBOOK QUESTIONS **EXERCISE 2**

1. Do you have three rings? Yes, I have three rings.
   No, I don't have three rings.
2. How many books do you have? I have ____ book(s).
   I don't have any books.
3. How many elephants do you have? I have ____ elephant(s).
   I don't have any elephants.
4. Where do you go after class? I go home after class.
   I go to _____ after class.
5. Do you go to town on Saturdays? Yes, I go to town on Saturdays.
   No, I don't go to town on Saturdays.
6. Did you play basketball last year? Yes, I played basketball last year.
   No, I didn't play basketball last year.
7. Did you eat supper at home yesterday? Yes, I ate supper at home yesterday.
   No I didn't eat supper at home yesterday.
8. Did you hike in the mountains last year? Yes, I hiked in the mountains last year.
   No, I didn't hike in the mountains last year.
9. Were you at the theater last night? Yes, I was at the theater last night.
   No, I wasn't at the theater last night.
10. Was your friend at your house last night? Yes, my friend was at my house last night.
    No, my friend wasn't at my house last night.

TEST 7 TOTAL MARKS: 50
ANSWERS TO THE TEST 7 QUESTIONS

1. What did Ruth play? Ruth *played* basketball.
2. When did she play basketball? *She played basketball yesterday afternoon.*
3. Did you play basketball yesterday? *Yes, I played basketball yesterday.*
   No, I didn't play basketball yesterday.
4. Did Raymond hike in the mountains last week? *Yes, Raymond hiked in the mountains last week.*
5. Was Raymond outside last week? *Yes, Raymond was outside last week.*
6. Were you outside last week? *Yes, I was outside last week.*
   No, I wasn't outside last week.

7. to watch – *watched*   11. to go - *went*   15. to eat – *ate*   19. to phone - *phoned*
8. to like - *liked*   12. to have – *had*   16. to meet – *met*   20. to close - *closed*
9. to want - *wanted*   13. to be (singular) - *was*   17. to buy - *bought*
10. to follow – *followed*   14. to be (plural) – *were*   18. to see - *saw*

21. phone, She, the, answered *She answered the phone.*
22. to, went, movies, the, They *They went to the movies.*
23. at, He, was, home *He was at home.*

Teacher Guide

TEST 7   LESSONS 25 TO 28

NAME: _____

Answer the questions in sentences. Look at the pictures. (4 marks each)

1. What did Ruth play?
   _____

2. When did she play basketball?
   _____

3. Did you play basketball yesterday?
   _____

yesterday afternoon

4. Did Raymond hike in the mountains last week?
   _____

5. Was Raymond outside last week?
   _____

6. Were you outside last week?
   _____

last week

WRITE THE PAST TENSE OF THESE VERBS. (1 mark each)

7. to watch   8. to like   9. to want   10. to follow
   _____   _____   _____   _____

11. to go   12. to have   13. to be (singular) 14. to be (plural)
    _____   _____   _____   _____

15. to eat   16. to meet   17. to buy   18. to see
    _____   _____   _____   _____

19. to phone   20. to close
    _____   _____

Put the words in sentence order. (4 marks each)

21. phone, She, the, answered   _____

22. to, went, movies, the, They _____

23. at, He, was, home   _____

Teacher Guide

Lesson 29

ORAL QUESTIONS

Did you attend a soccer game last night? Yes, I attended a soccer game last night.
No, I didn't attend a soccer game last night.

Did you practice basketball last week? Yes, I practiced basketball last week.
No, I didn't practice basketball last week.

Did you want to play soccer last year? Yes, I wanted to play soccer last year.
No, I didn't want to play soccer last year.

Did you hike last weekend? Yes, I hiked last weekend.
No, I didn't hike last weekend.

Did you enjoy a movie last night? Yes, I enjoyed a movie last night.
No, I didn't enjoy a movie last night.

Did you walk with your friend yesterday? Yes, I walked with my friend yesterday.
No, I didn't walk with my friend yesterday.

Were you at work yesterday? Yes, I was at work yesterday.
No, I wasn't at work yesterday.

Did you go to New York last January? Yes, I went to New York last January.
No, I didn't go to New York last January.

Did you post a letter yesterday? Yes, I posted a letter yesterday.
No, I didn't post a letter yesterday.

Did you begin breakfast at seven today? Yes, I began breakfast at seven today.
No, I began breakfast at _____ today.

When did you read a book? I read a book _____.
I didn't read any books. / I didn't read a book.

When did you study your English? I studied my English _____.
I didn't study my English.

What did you buy today? I bought a / some _____ today.
I didn't buy anything today.

When did you meet your friend? I met my friend at _____.
I didn't meet my friend.

Who did you see at work/school today? I saw _____ at work/school today.

Did you close the door? Yes, I closed the door.
No, I didn't close the door.

Are the stores closed on Sundays? Yes, the stores are closed on Sundays.
Some stores are closed on Sundays.

Did you arrive ten minutes ago? Yes, I arrived ten minutes ago.
No, I didn't arrive ten minutes ago.

Was it Sunday the day before yesterday? Yes, it was Sunday the day before yesterday.
No, it wasn't Sunday the day before yesterday.

Teacher Guide

Lesson 29 Continued

ORAL QUESTIONS CONTINUED

Were you in class the day before yesterday? *Yes, I was in class the day before yesterday.*
No, I wasn't in class the day before yesterday.

Did you live here two years ago? *Yes, I lived here two years ago.*
No, I didn't live here two years ago.

Did you find your friend last night? *Yes, I found my friend last night.*
No, I didn't find my friend last night.

To the teacher:
Some words are used with the past tense of a verb to give a specific time in the past. They can also give the time <u>from a past event to the present.</u> EXAMPLE: He saw her <u>ten minutes ago.</u>

PAGE 62 — ANSWERS TO THE WORKBOOK QUESTIONS. ACTIVITY 2
1. He/She walked to town / last week / an hour ago...
2. He/She saw his/her neighbor / an hour ago...
3. He/She bought a book last month / year...
4. He/She attended a theater last weekend / month...
5. He/She began English classes last year / month...
6. He/She walked through town last...
7. He/She phoned his/her friend / last...
8. He/She ate in a restaurant last...
9. He/She studied English last...

PAGE 62 — ANSWERS TO THE WORKBOOK QUESTIONS. EXERCISE 1
1. breakfast, He, today, cooked — *He cooked breakfast today.*
2. wrote, a, yesterday, letter, They — *They wrote a letter yesterday.*
3. Saturdays, hike, They, on — *They hike on Saturdays.*
4. TV, night, They, last, watched — *They watched TV last night.*
5. book, She, minute, a, closed, ago, the — *She closed the book a minute ago.*
6. followed, That, today, dog, them, home — *That dog followed them home today.*

PAGE 63 — ANSWERS TO THE WORKBOOK QUESTIONS EXERCISE 2
1. Yes, I came to class the day before yesterday. — *No, I didn't come to class the day...*
2. Yes, I studied English a year ago. — *No, I didn't study English a year ago.*
3. Yes, I ate breakfast three hours ago. — *No, I didn't eat breakfast three hours ago.*
4. Yes, I visited my friend the day before yesterday. — *No, I didn't visit my friend the day...*
5. Yes, I talked to a student ten minutes ago. — *No, I didn't talk to a student ten minutes ago.*
6. It was _____ the day before yesterday.
7. Yes, I phoned my friend twenty-four hours ago. — *No, I didn't phone my friend twenty-four...*
8. Yes, I ate in a restaurant the day before yesterday. — *No, I didn't eat in a restaurant the day...*
9. Yes, the stores are closed on Sundays. — *No, the stores aren't closed on Sundays.*

PAGES 63 AND 64 — ANSWERS TO THE BINGO ACTIVITY 3

to find	*found*	to attend	*attended*	to begin	*began*	to like	*liked*
to have	*had*	to live	*lived*	to meet	*met*	to run	*ran*
to buy	*bought*	to eat	*ate*	to want	*wanted*	to volunteer	*volunteered*
to follow	*followed*	to answer	*answered*	to enjoy	*enjoyed*	to study	*studied*
to come	*came*	to do	*did*	to go	*went*	to play	*played*
to see	*saw*	to sit	*sat*	to hike	*hiked*	to put	*put*

Teacher Guide

Lesson 29 Continued

ACTIVITY 4

Divide the students into two groups and have them ask each other these questions.

Did you walk to class today?
Yes, I walked to class today.
No, I didn't walk to class today.

Did you buy a hamburger last week?
Yes, I bought a hamburger last week.
No, I didn't buy a hamburger last week.

Did you come to class last week?
Yes, I came to class last week.
No, I didn't come to class last week.

Did you attend the theater last year?
Yes, I attended the theater last year.
No, I didn't attend the theater last year.

Did you eat dinner at home yesterday?
Yes, I ate dinner at home yesterday.
No, I didn't eat dinner at home yesterday.

Were you at the theater last week?
Yes, I was at the theater last week.
No, I wasn't at the theater last week.

Did you have a hamburger today?
Yes, I had a hamburger today.
No, I didn't have a hamburger today.

Did you find your pen?
Yes, I found my pen.
No, I didn't find my pen.

Did you see your friend today?
Yes, I saw my friend today.
No, I didn't see my friend today

Was your dog outside today?
Yes, my dog was outside today.
No, my dog wasn't outside today.

Were you with your friend today?
Yes, I was with my friend today.
No, I wasn't with my friend today.

Where did you put your book?
I put my book on...

Did you buy an apple yesterday?
Yes, I bought an apple yesterday.
No, I didn't buy an apple yesterday.

Did you play basketball last week?
Yes, I played basketball last week.
No, I didn't play basketball last week.

Did you see a dog today?
Yes, I saw a dog today.
No, I didn't see a dog today.

Did you meet your father today?
Yes, I met my father today.
No, I didn't meet my father today.

Teacher Guide

Lesson 30

To the teacher:
When you add "ing" to a word that ends in a single silent "e" drop the "e" before adding "ing"

have - having

For the form "studying" do not change the "y" in the word "study"
because you are adding an ending that begins with "i".
Always leave the "y" when you add any ending that begins with "i".   (studying)

ORAL QUESTIONS

Are you playing soccer today?	*Yes, I'm playing soccer today.*
	No, I'm not playing soccer today.
Are you practicing basketball now?	*Yes, I'm practicing basketball now.*
	No, I'm not practicing basketball now.
Are you writing a letter now?	*Yes, I'm writing a letter now.*
	No, I'm not writing a letter now.
Are you learning English now?	*Yes, I'm learning English now.*
	No, I'm not learning English now.
Are you using a dictionary now?	*Yes, I'm using a dictionary now.*
	No, I'm not using a dictionary now.
Are you phoning a friend now?	*Yes, I'm phoning a friend now.*
	No, I'm not phoning a friend now.
Are you partying now?	*Yes, I'm partying now.*
	No, I'm not partying now.
Did you have a good day yesterday?	*Yes, I had a good day yesterday.*
	No, I didn't have a good day yesterday.
Did you go to the theater yesterday?	*Yes, I went to the theater yesterday.*
	No, I didn't go to the theater yesterday.
Did you go to school yesterday?	*Yes, I went to school yesterday.*
	No, I didn't go to school yesterday.
Did you eat supper yesterday?	*Yes, I ate supper yesterday.*
	No, I didn't eat supper yesterday.

PAGE 65   **ANSWERS TO THE WORKBOOK QUESTIONS**   **EXERCISE 1:**

1. *He is playing soccer now*
2. *No, I'm not playing soccer now.*
3. *I am learning English now.*
4. *My friend is learning English (now), too.*

Teacher Guide

Lesson 31

PAGE 65 — ANSWERS TO THE WORKBOOK QUESTIONS — **EXERCISE 2**

1. He is *phoning* her every day. (phone)
2. They are *hiking* on Saturdays. (hike)
3. They are *practicing* soccer now. (practice)
4. The man was *watching* them. (watch)
5. He is *using* a dictionary. (use)
6. She is *writing* a letter. (write)
7. They are *doing* some volunteer work. (do)

PAGE 65 — ANSWERS TO THE WORKBOOK QUESTIONS — **EXERCISE 3**

1. She is *trying* to sew. (try)
2. They are *partying* all night with their friends. (party)
3. They are *frying* the fish. (fry)
4. The friends are *enjoying* the beach. (enjoy)
5. The students are *studying* English. (study)
6. The plane is *flying* to Bombay. (fly)
7. He is *crying*. (cry)
8. They enjoy *playing* soccer. (play)

PAGE 66 — ANSWERS TO THE WORKBOOK QUESTIONS — **EXERCISE 4**

1. Nancy eats breakfast. — *Nancy is eating breakfast.*
2. Ming has Chinese food for dinner. — *Ming is having Chinese food for dinner.*
3. Raymond rides a bicycle. — *Raymond is riding a bicycle.*
4. Craig cooks supper. — *Craig is cooking supper.*
5. It rains outside. — *It is raining outside.*
6. Jessica enjoys the snow. — *Jessica is enjoying the snow.*
7. Ruth reads a book. — *Ruth is reading a book.*
8. I study English now. — *I am studying English now.*
9. Nancy wears a pair of gloves. — *Nancy is wearing a pair of gloves.*

PAGE 66 — ANSWERS TO THE WORKBOOK QUESTIONS — **ACTIVITY 1**

1. ___ (name) is from ____.
2. _____ has one face.
3. Yes, __ has a dress.
   No, __ doesn't have a dress.
4. Yes, _____ is from Canada.
   No, _____ isn't from Canada.
5. The desk is in front of _____.
6. ___ came to class at ____. (time)
7. ____'s house is on _____ Street.
8. _____ is with _____
9. __ comes to English classes on __ and __.
10. __ lives at __ __ Street. (number and street name.)
11. _____ walked to class today.
    _____ didn't walk to class today.

PAGE 66 — ANSWERS TO THE WORKBOOK QUESTIONS — **EXERCISE 5**

1. Where is Peter? — *Peter is at Sarah's house.*
2. How is Peter? — *Peter is hungry.*
3. How does Sarah look? — *Sarah (She) looks great.*
4. Do you like Chinese food? — *Yes, I like Chinese food. / No, I don't like…*

LESSON 31

ORAL QUESTIONS

Review all oral questions from Lessons 25 and 26.

Did a dog follow you today?	*Yes, a dog followed me today.* *No, a dog didn't follow me today.*
Are you eating dinner now?	*No, I'm not eating dinner now.*
Is it dinner time now?	*Yes, it's dinner time now.* *No, it isn't dinner time now.*
Are you listening to music?	*Yes, I'm listening to music.* *No, I'm not listening to music.*
Is your friend sleeping now?	*Yes, my friend is sleeping now.* *No, my friend isn't sleeping now.*
Are you writing in your notebook?	*Yes, I'm writing in my notebook.* *No, I'm not writing in my notebook.*
Are you usually using computers at work?	*Yes, I'm (usually) using computers at work.* *No, I'm not (usually) using computers at work.*
Are you having a day off today?	*Yes, I'm having a day off today.* *No, I'm not having a day off today.*
Are you having Chinese food today?	*Yes, I'm having Chinese food today.* *No, I'm not having Chinese food today.*
Are you wearing a pair of gloves?	*Yes, I'm wearing a pair of gloves.* *No, I'm not wearing a pair of gloves.*
Are you wearing a pair of shoes?	*Yes, I'm wearing a pair of shoes.* *No, I'm not wearing a pair of shoes.*
Did you eat breakfast today?	*Yes, I ate breakfast today.* *No, I didn't eat breakfast today.*
Did you cook dinner yesterday?	*Yes, I cooked dinner yesterday.* *No, I didn't cook dinner yesterday.*
Do you have two feet?	*Yes, I have two feet.*
Did you run to class today?	*Yes, I ran to class today.* *No, I didn't run to class today.*
Did it rain today?	*Yes, it rained today.* *No, it didn't rain today.*
Do you have another English class today?	*Yes, I have another English class today.* *No, I don't have another English class today.*
Did you have a party last night?	*Yes, I had a party last night.* *No, I didn't have a party last night.*
Did you phone your friend today?	*Yes, I phoned my friend today.* *No, I didn't phone my friend today.*

Teacher Guide

Lesson 31 Continued

PAGE 67 — ANSWERS TO THE WORKBOOK QUESTIONS — **EXERCISE 1**

Add _ing_ to these words:

put - *putting*   swim - *swimming*   stop - *stopping*

PAGE 67 — ANSWERS TO THE WORKBOOK QUESTIONS — **EXERCISE 2**

Add _ing_ to these words:

eat - *eating*   wear - *wearing*
cook - *cooking*   rain - *raining*

PAGE 67 — ANSWERS TO THE WORKBOOK QUESTIONS — **EXERCISE 3**

Add –ed to these words:

cook - *cooked*   look - *looked*   rain - *rained*

PAGE 67 — ANSWERS TO THE WORKBOOK QUESTIONS — **EXERCISE 4**

1. It is *raining* outside.
2. He is *cooking* dinner.
3. It *rained* yesterday.
4. She is *meeting* her friend.
5. They are *sitting* at the table.
6. She is *putting* her book on the table.
7. He is *stopping* at the corner.
8. She is *swimming* in the water.
9. They are *meeting* their friends.
10. Are you *wearing* a coat?
11. The car *stopped* at the corner.

PAGE 67 — ANSWERS TO THE WORKBOOK QUESTIONS — **EXERCISE 5**

use / *using*   write - *writing*   ride / *riding*   have - *having*
come - *coming*   phone - *phoning*   close - *closing*   arrive - *arriving*

PAGE 68 — ANSWERS TO THE WORKBOOK QUESTIONS — **EXERCISE 6**

1. Are you practicing basketball now?   No, I'm not practicing basketball now.
2. Are you reading a book?   Yes, I'm reading a book.
3. Is your mother living in this city?   Yes, my mother is living in this city.
    No, my mother isn't living in this city.
4. Are you wearing a T-shirt today?   Yes, I'm wearing a T-shirt today.
    No, I'm not wearing a T-shirt today.
5. Are you talking to a friend?   Yes, I'm talking to a friend. / No, I'm not talking to a...
6. Are you eating dinner?   No, I'm not eating dinner.

PAGE 68 — ANSWERS TO THE WORKBOOK QUESTIONS — **EXERCISE 7**

1. We are in the classroom.
2. He listens to the radio.
3. They go to work.
4. He is wearing blue jeans.
5. They are frying a fish.
6. They arrived the day before yesterday.
7. She ate breakfast ten minutes ago.
8. She wasn't at home.
9. He was laughing.
10. She wrote in her notebook.

PAGE 69 — ANSWERS TO THE BINGO — **ACTIVITY 2**

15	lunch	8	to stop	18	sleep	21	sure
4	days off	3	pair of shoes	12	notebook	11	work
7	pair of gloves	2	Chinese food	23	television	16	feet
17	plane (airplane)	14	fish	6	to fry	24	mango juice
1	weekend	13	store	5	breakfast	19	an hour
20	inside	10	library	9	pictures	22	game

Teacher Guide

Lesson 32 - Review

Review oral questions from Lessons 29, 30, and 31 if the students need extra practice.
ACTIVITY 2   Divide into two teams. Follow the directions on Page 93 of this guide.

How are you today?
I'm fine. / I'm just great. / I'm doing fine / I'm okay
I'm so-so / I'm not so good. / I'm not very well

Do you have a notebook?
Yes, I have a notebook.
No, I don't have a notebook.

Do you sometimes paint pictures?
Yes, I sometimes paint pictures.
No, I don't paint pictures.

Are you laughing now?
Yes, I'm laughing now.
No, I'm not laughing now.

Do you have two feet?
Yes, I have two feet.

Do you have a pair gloves?
Yes, I have a pair of gloves.
No, I don't have a pair of gloves.

Is it raining now?
Yes, it's raining now.
No, it isn't raining now.

Do you like eating fish?
Yes, I like eating fish.
No, I don't like eating fish.

Did you practice archery last weekend?
Yes, I practiced archery last weekend.
No, I didn't practice archery last weekend.

Did you put your book on the table?
Yes, I put my book on the table.
No, I didn't put my book on the table.

Did you go to work today?
Yes, I went to work today.
No, I didn't go to work today.

Are you listening to the radio now?
Yes, I'm listening to the radio now.
No, I'm not listening to the radio now.

Are you having a day-off today?
Yes, I'm having a day off today.
No, I'm not having a day off today.

Do you sleep at night?
Yes, I sleep at night.
No, I don't sleep at night.

Do airplanes fly?
Yes, airplanes fly.

Are you wearing a T-shirt today?
Yes, I'm wearing a T-shirt today.
No, I'm not wearing a T-shirt today.

Do you study English every day?
Yes, I study English every day.
No, I don't study English every day.

Did you watch television last night?
Yes, I watched television last night.
No, I didn't watch television last night.

Did you live here last year?
Yes, I lived here last year.
No, I didn't live here last year.

Did you eat dinner yesterday?
Yes, I ate dinner yesterday.
No, I didn't eat dinner yesterday.

Teacher Guide

Lesson 32 - Continued

PAGE 70   **ANSWERS TO THE WORKBOOK QUESTIONS**   **EXERCISE 1**

1. Craig and Jessica go to the theatre on Friday nights.
2. Yes, Raymond is practicing archery three times a week.
3. Yes, Ruth is playing on a school team.
4. Toto is at home (on Friday nights.)
5. Toto is sleeping.
6. Yes, I go to a restaurant on Friday nights. / No, I don't go to a restaurant on Friday nights.

PAGE 70   **ANSWERS TO THE WORKBOOK QUESTIONS**   **EXERCISE 2**

Answering in the present progressive tense:

1. No, I'm not watching television now.
2. No, I'm not eating lunch in a restaurant now.
3. Yes, my friend is looking out the window now.
   No, my friend isn't looking out the window now.
4. I'm studying English now.
5. No, I'm not sleeping now.
6. No, I'm not drinking mango juice now.

PAGE 71   **ANSWERS TO THE WORKBOOK QUESTIONS**   **EXERCISE 3**

1. He is crying.
2. They are frying the fish.
3. She is talking on the phone.
4. He is playing soccer.
5. He is practicing archery.
6. I'm practicing…

TEST 8 TOTAL MARKS: 50
ORAL QUESTIONS FOR TEST 8   LESSONS 29 to 32

QUESTIONS ANSWERS (4 marks each)

1. Did you eat lunch yesterday?   Yes, I ate lunch yesterday.
   No, I didn't eat lunch yesterday.
2. Are you painting a picture now?   No, I'm not painting a picture now.
3. What country are you living in?   I'm living in _____.
4. Did you walk to class today?   Yes, I walked to class today.
   No, I didn't walk to class today.
5. Did you see your friend last night?   Yes, I saw my friend last night.
   No, I didn't see my friend last night.

ANSWERS TO THE TEST 8 QUESTIONS (4 marks each)

6. Is the car stopping?   Yes, the car is stopping.
7. Is she wearing a dress?   Yes, she is wearing a dress.
8. Today is Thursday.
   What day was it the day before yesterday?   It was Tuesday the day before yesterday.
9. Are you writing a test now?   Yes, I'm writing a test now.
10. Are you sleeping now?   No, I'm not sleeping now.
11. Do airplanes fly?   Yes, airplanes fly.
12. Do you like Chinese food?   Yes, I like Chinese food.
    No, I don't like Chinese food.

13.   The days of the weekend are *Saturday* and *Sunday*. (1 mark each word)

Teacher Guide

TEST 8   LESSONS 29 to 32

NAME: _____

Write the answers to the oral questions here: (4 marks each)

1. _____

2. _____

3. _____

4. _____

5. _____

6. Is the car stopping?

   _____

7. Is she wearing a dress?

   _____

Answer in a sentence. (4 marks each)

8. Today is Thursday. What day was it the day before yesterday?

   _____

9. Are you writing a test now?

   _____

10. Are you sleeping now?

    _____

11. Do airplanes fly?

    _____

12. Do you like Chinese food?

    _____

13. The days of the weekend are _____ and _____. (1 mark each word)

    Sunday   Monday   Tuesday   Wednesday   Thursday   Friday   Saturday

Teacher Guide

LESSON 33

Note to the teacher: Pants made of heavy cotton are <u>blue jeans</u> but they are usually called <u>jeans</u>.

ORAL QUESTIONS

Were you listening to the radio yesterday?   *Yes, I was listening to the radio yesterday.*
No, I wasn't listening to the radio yesterday.

Was it raining yesterday?   *Yes, it was raining yesterday.*
No, it wasn't raining yesterday.

Were you cooking dinner last night?   *Yes, I was cooking dinner last night.*
No, I wasn't cooking dinner last night.

Were you driving a car today?   *Yes, I was driving a car today.*
No, I wasn't driving a car today.

Were you watching TV last night?   *Yes, I was watching TV last night.*
No, I wasn't watching TV last night.

Were you working yesterday?   *Yes, I was working yesterday.*
No, I wasn't working yesterday.

Were you seeing your friend last night?   *Yes, I was seeing my friend last night.*
No, I wasn't seeing my friend last night.

Were you wearing a hat this morning?   *Yes, I was wearing a hat this morning.*
No, I wasn't wearing a hat this morning.

Were you wearing blue jeans yesterday?   *Yes, I was wearing blue jeans yesterday.*
No, I wasn't wearing blue jeans yesterday.

Were you drinking juice the day before yesterday?   *Yes, I was drinking juice the day before…*
No, I wasn't drinking juice the day before…

Were you riding an elephant today?   *Yes, I was riding an elephant today.*
No, I wasn't riding an elephant today.

Were you listening to <u>some</u> music last week?   *Yes, I was listening to <u>some</u> music last week.*
No, I wasn't listening to <u>any</u> music last week.

Were you sleeping last night?   *Yes, I was sleeping last night.*
No, I wasn't sleeping last night.

Was your friend giving a party last week?   *Yes, my friend was giving a party last week.*
No, my friend wasn't giving a party last week.

Were you reading <u>some</u> books last month?   *Yes, I was reading <u>some</u> books last month.*
No, I wasn't reading <u>any</u> books last month.

Were you walking in the park last night?   *Yes, I was walking in the park last night.*
No, I wasn't walking in the park last night.

Were you watching <u>some</u> birds last week?   *Yes, I was watching <u>some</u> birds last week.*
No, I wasn't watching <u>any</u> birds last week.

Were you wearing a long dress this morning?   *Yes, I was wearing a long dress this morning.*
No, I wasn't wearing a long dress this morning.

Teacher Guide

Lesson 33 Continued

PAGE 58 **ANSWERS TO THE STUDENT READER QUESTIONS** **ACTIVITY 1**

1. What are they doing? — *They are hiking in the mountains.*
2. Where are they going? — *They are going to the park.*
3. What are they watching? — *They are watching archery.*

PAGE 72 **ANSWERS TO THE WORKBOOK QUESTIONS** **EXERCISE 1**

1. *Ruth was playing basketball yesterday morning.*
2. *I was playing basketball last night.*
   I wasn't playing basketball last night.
3. *I was _____ yesterday.*
4. *Yes, it was snowing last week.*
   No, it wasn't snowing last week.
5. *Yes, I was practicing archery the day before yesterday.*
   No, I wasn't practicing archery the day before yesterday.

PAGE 72 **ANSWERS TO THE WORKBOOK QUESTIONS** **EXERCISE 2**

1. Craig drove his car to work last week. — *Craig was driving his car to work last week.*
2. Ruth rode her bicycle to school today. — *Ruth was riding her bicycle to school today.*
3. Nancy bought a pair of shoes. — *Nancy was buying a pair of shoes.*
4. Raymond wore a pair of gloves. — *Raymond was wearing a pair of gloves.*
5. Craig and Jessica went to a movie. — *Craig and Jessica were going to a movie.*
6. Ming practiced soccer last week. — *Ming was practicing soccer last week.*
7. They lived in Australia last year. — *They were living in Australia last year.*
8. She came to school. — *She was coming to school.*
9. They hiked through the snow. — *They were hiking through the snow.*
10. They volunteered at the hospital. — *They were volunteering at the hospital.*

PAGE 73 **ANSWERS TO THE WORKBOOK QUESTIONS** **EXERCISE 3**

1. Was your friend laughing this morning? — *Yes, my friend was laughing this morning.*
   No, my friend wasn't laughing this morning.
2. Were you wearing a jacket yesterday? — *Yes, I was wearing a jacket yesterday.*
   No, I wasn't wearing a jacket yesterday.
3. Was your teacher wearing a long dress this morning — *Yes, my teacher was wearing...*
   No, my teacher wasn't wearing ...
4. Were you eating an apple last night? — *Yes, I was eating an apple last night.*
   No, I wasn't eating an apple last night.
5. Were you walking through town yesterday afternoon? — *Yes, I was walking through town yesterday afternoon.*
   No, I wasn't walking through...

Teacher Guide

Lesson 33 Continued

ACTIVITY 3   THE PAST TENSE   (DIRECTIONS)

Give each student <u>one role card</u> that describes a friend they had five years ago.
They are to ask two other students the questions on the information card.
Then they are to write the student's answers using reported speech.

EXAMPLE: What was your friend's name?   *His / Her name was _____.*

ANDREW DONOVAN (5 years ago)
Nationality - Past: Vietnamese
Activity - walking
Days off - Mondays and Tuesdays

SALLY RAY (5 years ago)
Nationality - Past: Australian
Activity - running
Days off - Saturdays and Sundays

KIM RHODES (5 years ago)
Nationality - Past: Greek
Activity – soccer
Days off - Mondays and Tuesdays

MARIE McLAREN (5 years ago)
Nationality - Past: South African
Activity - driving
Days off - Tuesdays and Wednesdays

JOHN MUNROE (5 years ago)
Nationality - Past: Israeli
Activity - basketball
Days off - Sundays and Mondays

MICHAEL ASHTON (5 years ago)
Nationality - Past: French
Activity - swimming
Days off - Fridays and Saturdays

JEAN RUSSELL (5 years ago)
Nationality - Past: American
Activity - writing
Days off - Thursdays and Fridays

MARK NORMAN (5 years ago)
Nationality - Past: Russian
Activity - swimming
Days off - Sundays and Mondays

Teacher Guide

Lesson 33 Continued

LINDA WATTS (5 years ago)
Nationality - Past: American
Activity - hiking
Days off - Fridays and Saturdays

MARGARET SELKIRK (5 years ago)
Nationality - Past: Indian
Activity - reading
Days off - Sundays and Mondays

JOSEPH WOODS (5 years ago)
Nationality - Past: Canadian
Activity - swimming
Days off - Thursdays and Fridays

SAM MUNN (5 years ago)
Nationality - Past: Australian
Activity - driving
Days off - Tuesdays and Wednesdays

ALAN DUNNING (5 years ago)
Nationality - Past: British
Activity – soccer
Days off - Fridays and Saturdays

ELIZABETH FRASER (5 years ago)
Nationality - Past: Canadian
Activity - walking
Days off - Thursdays and Fridays

MIRANDA BATES (5 years ago)
Nationality - Past: Mexican
Activity – practicing archery
Days off - Sundays and Mondays

BETTY BLACK (5 years ago)
Nationality - Past: Czech
Activity- swimming
Days off - Fridays and Saturdays

Teacher Guide

Lesson 34

Note to the teacher: In North America we eat a small meal at noon, which we call lunch. We have our bigger meal around 6 PM (18:00). This is called dinner.

ORAL QUESTIONS

Are you wearing a dress today?

Yes, I am wearing a dress today.
No, I am not wearing a dress today.

Are you studying English now?

Yes, I am studying English now.
No, I am not studying English now.

Is your mother working today?

Yes, my mother is working today.
No, she is not working today.

Are you writing in your book?

Yes, I'm writing in my book.
No, I'm not writing in my book.

Are you sitting in / on a chair?

Yes, I'm sitting on / in a chair.
No, I'm not sitting on / in a chair.

Were you eating at home this morning?

Yes, I was eating at home this morning.
No, I wasn't eating at home this morning.

Were you driving a car today?

Yes, I was driving a car today.
No, I wasn't driving a car today.

Was your mother cooking supper last night?

Yes, my mother was cooking supper last night.
No, she wasn't cooking supper last night.

Were you sleeping at midnight?

Yes, I was sleeping at midnight.
No, I wasn't sleeping at midnight.

Were you phoning your friend this afternoon?

Yes, I was phoning my friend this afternoon.
No, I wasn't phoning my friend this afternoon.

Were you talking to your family at supper?

Yes, I was talking to my family at supper.
No, I wasn't talking to my family at supper.

Were you working in the afternoon?

Yes, I was working in the afternoon.
No, I wasn't working in the afternoon.

Did you return home late last night?

Yes, I returned home late last night.
No, I didn't return home late last night.

Do you go to a restaurant after work?

Yes, I go to a restaurant after work.
No, I don't go to a restaurant after work..

Do you listen to the radio at night?

Yes, I listen to the radio at night.
No, I don't listen to the radio at night.

Do you have some things on your desk?

Yes, I have some things on my desk.
No, I don't have anything on my desk.

Did your friend visit you yesterday?

Yes, my friend visited me yesterday.
No, my friend didn't visit me yesterday.

Were you eating in a restaurant last night?

Yes, I was eating in a restaurant last night.
No, I wasn't eating in a restaurant last night.

Is there a lake nearby?

Yes, there is a lake nearby.
No, there isn't a lake nearby.

Teacher Guide

Lesson 34 Continued

ACTIVITY 3
Divide the students into two groups and have them ask each other these questions.

Did you find your friend?
Yes, I found my friend.
No, I didn't find my friend.

Did you answer your telephone yesterday?
Yes, I answered my telephone yesterday.
No, I didn't answer my telephone yesterday.

Were you swimming at a lake yesterday?
Yes, I was swimming at a lake yesterday.
No, I wasn't swimming at a lake yesterday.

Did you walk home after class last week?
Yes, I walked home after class last week.
No, I didn't walk home after class last week.

Do you live nearby?
Yes, I live nearby.
No, I don't live nearby.

Are the stores closed on Saturdays?
Yes, the stores are closed on Saturdays.
No, the stores aren't closed on Saturdays.

What did you buy today?
I bought a / some _____.
I didn't buy anything.

Were you talking to your friend today?
Yes, I was talking to my friend.
No, I wasn't talking to my friend.

Did your friend phone you today?
Yes, my friend phoned me today.
No, my friend didn't phone me today.

Did you enjoy the theater last week?
Yes, I enjoyed the theater last week.
No, I didn't enjoy the theater last week.

Did you close the door when you came in?
Yes, I closed the door.
No, I didn't close the door.

Did you return home late last night?
Yes, I returned home late last night.
No, I didn't return home late last night.

How many books did you read last week?
I read _____ books.
I didn't read any books.

Were you late for class today?
Yes, I was late for class today.
No, I wasn't late for class today.

Who did you meet yesterday?
I met my friend.
I didn't meet anyone.

Did you wear a pair of shoes today?
Yes, I wore a pair of shoes today.
No, I didn't wear a pair of shoes today.

Teacher Guide

Lesson 34 Continued

PAGE 74   ANSWERS TO THE WORKBOOK QUESTIONS   **EXERCISE 1**

1. When do you eat breakfast?   *I eat breakfast in the morning.*
2. When do you go to sleep?   *I go to sleep at night. / at midnight.*
3. When do you see your friends?   *I see my friends in the evening / at night…*
4. When do you eat dinner in San Francisco?   *We / I eat dinner at noon / in the evening.*
5. When do you go to work / school?   *I go to work / school in the morning / in the afternoon…*
6. When do you eat lunch?   *I eat lunch at noon / in the afternoon.*
7. When do you sleep?   *I sleep at night / in the evening.*

PAGE 74   ANSWERS TO THE WORKBOOK QUESTIONS   **EXERCISE 2**

Raymond and his friend Ming did many things last year. They often hiked in the mountains **on** Saturdays and they usually went to a lake to swim **on** Sundays. Sometimes they went out **with** their friends to a restaurant. After dinner, they returned home late **in** the evening and went to bed **at** midnight.

PAGE 74   ANSWERS TO THE WORKBOOK QUESTIONS   **EXERCISE 3**

park	a quiet place with many trees
breakfast	you eat it in the morning
music	you listen to it
fly	airplanes do it
hungry	you want something to eat
shoes	you wear them on your feet

PAGE 75   ANSWERS TO THE WORKBOOK QUESTIONS   **EXERCISE 4**

1. Wednesday comes after Tuesday.
2. August comes after July.
3. Monday comes after Sunday.
4. The last four months are September, October, November and December.
5. My birthday is _____
6. Christmas is in December.
7. I eat supper _____.
8. Yes, I like to get up in the morning. No I don't like to get up in the morning.
9. Yes, I am sometimes late for class. No, I am never late for class.
10. Yes, I sometimes sleep late on Sunday mornings. No, I don't ever sleep late on …

PAGES 123 – 125 GUIDE   BARBARA AND BILL: (DIRECTIONS)   **ACTIVITY 4**

Photocopy the sixteen pictures and the story.
Give each student **one** picture **and** the story of Barbara and Bill.
If there are more students than pictures, give the last two pictures out twice.

The students are to:
Decide which sentence matches their picture.
Find another student with a picture that matches their sentence. (Underlined words are clues.)
Each pair is to read their sentence(s) to the group starting at the beginning of the story.
Write the story in the past tense. Read the story in the past tense.

Teacher Guide

Lesson 34 Continued

THE STORY OF BARBARA AND BILL

Barbara and Bill are friends.
They talk on the telephone every day.
Bill goes to work at seven o'clock. Barbara is at work a six o'clock.
On Saturday night, they go to the movies. They get to the cinema at seven o'clock.
On Sundays they go for a walk with Barbara's dog.
Sometimes they watch television. (2 pictures)
Sometimes they swim. (2 pictures)
Barbara and Bill are happy. (2 pictures)

Teacher Guide

Lesson 34 Continued

Lesson 34 Continued

Teachers Guide

Lesson 35

To the teacher:
Grammar: The use of "will" and "going to" to express the future.
In common speech the grammatical rules are flexible.
To help the students, we will introduce "will" in this lesson and "going to" in the following lesson.
Please note that the friends are making a plan, not talking about a plan that they made in the past.
"Will" is especially used to express willingness. <u>Will you answer the phone?</u>
It is also used to talk about something that might happen in the future.

let
"**Let**" is used as an auxiliary verb without the "to".
It is used to make a suggestion. **EXAMPLE:**   Let us go = **Let's go**

ORAL QUESTIONS

Will you help your friend tonight?
    Yes, I will help my friend tonight.
    No, I won't help my friend tonight.

Will you be able to have a holiday next month?
    Yes, I'll be able to have a holiday next month.
    No, I won't be able to have a holiday next month.

Will you answer the phone?
    Yes, I'll answer the phone.
    No, I won't answer the phone.

Will it rain tomorrow?
    Yes, it will rain tomorrow.
    No, it won't rain tomorrow.

Will you come to the party?
    Yes, I'll come to the party.
    No, I won't come to the party.

Will you have some juice?
    Yes, I'll have some juice.
    No, I won't have any juice.

Will you stay at a hotel?
    Yes, I'll stay at a hotel.
    No, I won't stay at a hotel.

Do you know of a good hotel?
    Yes, I know of a good hotel.
    No, I don't know of a good hotel.

Will you visit your friends next month?
    Yes, I'll visit my friends next month.
    No, I won't visit my friends next month.

Will you close the door please?
    Yes, I'll close the door.
    No, I won't close the door.
    No, I won't be able to close the door.

Will you visit a big city next year?
    Yes, I'll visit a big city next year.
    No, I won't visit a big city next year.

Will you have some apple juice?
    Yes, I'll have some apple juice.
    No, I won't have any apple juice.

Will you give me your book?
    Yes, I'll give you my book.
    No, I won't give you my book.
    No, I won't be able to give you my book.

Teachers Guide

Lesson 35 Continued

ANSWERS TO THE STUDENT READER QUESTIONS

PAGE 61 — **ACTIVITY 1**

It is cold in the mountains
There are many birds in the trees.
They hike through the snow.
They see their friends on Saturday night.

It will be cold in the mountains.
There will be many birds in the trees.
They will hike through the snow.
They will see their friends on Saturday night.

PAGE 76 — **ANSWERS TO THE WORKBOOK QUESTIONS** — **EXERCISE 1**

1. *He will play soccer.*
2. *She will drive the car to town.*
3. *They will practice basketball.*
4. *They will hike all day.*
5. *The boys will eat chicken.*
6. *She will wear a pair of gloves.*
7. *It will rain outside.*
8. *She will look for a pair of shoes.*
9. *He will begin English classes.*
10. *She will know the answer.*

PAGE 76 — **ANSWERS TO THE WORKBOOK QUESTIONS** — **EXERCISE 2**

1. *I will go to _____ tomorrow*
2. *I will go to Delhi in _____.*
   I won't go to Delhi.
3. *I will find my friend (in / at) _____.*
4. *I will see _____ tomorrow.*
5. *I will see _____ in the store.*
6. *I will eat breakfast at home.*

PAGE 77 — **ANSWERS TO THE WORKBOOK QUESTIONS** — **EXERCISE 3**

1. *When will you go (to) ____?*
2. *Where will you live?*
3. *How will you know?*
4. *Who will you meet?*
5. *Where will you hike?*
6. *Where will you stay?*

PAGE 77 — **ANSWERS TO THE WORKBOOK QUESTIONS** — **EXERCISE 4**

1. Who wanted a holiday? — *Luke and Rose wanted to have a holiday.*
2. Will they go to Delhi? — *Yes, they'll go to Delhi.*
3. How will they get to Delhi? — *They'll get there by bus.*
   They'll go by bus.
4. Where will they stay in Delhi? — *They'll stay at / in / the Peace Hotel.*
5. Where will they meet? — *They'll meet on the bus.*
6. Who will phone for a hotel reservation? — *Rose will phone for a hotel reservation.*
7. Which hotel will she phone? — *She'll phone the Peace Hotel.*

Teachers Guide

Lesson 36

ORAL QUESTIONS

Were you inside a church/mosque/temple yesterday?	Yes, I was inside a _____ yesterday.
	No, I wasn't inside a _____ yesterday.
Were you walking through town this morning?	Yes, I was walking through town this morning.
	No, I wasn't walking through town this morning.
Are you wearing blue jeans?	Yes, I'm wearing blue jeans.
	No, I'm not wearing blue jeans.
Were you talking to your friend this morning?	Yes, I was talking to my friend this morning.
	No, I wasn't talking to my friend this morning.
Is it raining outside?	Yes, it's raining outside.
	No, it isn't raining outside.
Are you wearing warm clothes?	Yes, I'm wearing warm clothes.
	No, I'm not wearing warm clothes.
Is this the month of April?	Yes, it's the month of April.
	No, it isn't the month of April.
Will you return home tonight?	Yes, I will (I'll) return home tonight.
	No, I will not (won't) return home tonight.
Are you usually sleeping at midnight?	Yes, I'm usually sleeping at midnight.
	No, I'm not usually sleeping ay midnight.
Do you live nearby?	Yes, I live nearby.
	No, I don't live nearby.
Did you meet anyone on your way to school?	Yes, I met someone on my way to school.
	No, I didn't meet anyone on my way to school.
Do you have something on your desk?	Yes, I have something on my desk.
	No, I don't have anything on my desk.
Were you late for class this morning?	Yes, I was late for class this morning.
	No, I wasn't late for class this morning.
Were you eating your lunch at noon yesterday?	Yes, I was eating my lunch at noon yesterday.
	No, I wasn't eating my lunch at noon yesterday.
Will you go to bed tonight?	Yes, I'll go to bed tonight.
	No, I won't go to bed tonight.
Will you go to Delhi next year?	Yes, I'll go to Delhi next year.
	No, I won't go to Delhi next year.
Will you have a holiday this week?	Yes, I'll have a holiday this week.
	No, I won't have a holiday this week.
Will you stay at a hotel tonight?	Yes, I'll stay at a hotel tonight.
	No, I won't stay at a hotel tonight.
Did Gandhi work for peace?	Yes, Gandhi worked for peace.

Teachers Guide

Lesson 36 Continued

PAGE 63   SOME ANSWERS TO THE STUDENT READER QUESTIONS   **ACTIVITY 2**

1. Where is Mahatma Gandhi's Memorial?   *It's in Delhi.*
2. Did you go to Gandhi's Memorial last year?   *Yes, I went to… / No, I didn't go to…*
3. Did Gandhi work for peace?   *Yes, Gandhi worked for peace.*
4. Does the Memorial have a garden?   *Yes, it has a big garden.*

PAGE 78   ANSWERS TO THE WORKBOOK QUESTIONS   **EXERCISE 1**

1. Where did the two couples go?   *They went to Delhi.*
2. Where did they go to check-in?   *They went to the front desk of the hotel.*
3. What are their surnames?   *Their surnames are Smith and Jones.*
4. Who gave them the keys to their rooms?   *The receptionist gave them the keys to their rooms.*
5. Where were their rooms?   *Their rooms were on the second floor.*
6. Who showed them to their rooms?   *The receptionist showed them to their rooms.*
7. Where did they eat breakfast?   *They ate breakfast in the restaurant.*
8. What does Luke want to see?   *He wants to see Gandhi's Memorial.*
9. How will they get to Gandhi's Memorial?   *They will go by taxi.*

PAGE 78   ANSWERS TO THE WORKBOOK QUESTIONS   **EXERCISE 2**

Sunday	*the first day of the week*	February	*the second month of the year*
March	*the third month of the year*	July	*the seventh month*
December	*the last month of the year*	April	*the fourth month of the year*
Saturday and Sunday	*the weekend*	Wednesday	*the middle of the week*

PAGE 79   ANSWERS TO THE WORKBOOK QUESTIONS   **EXERCISE 3**

1. Rose, Luke, Carol and Tom <u>arrive</u> at the Peace Hotel in Delhi. They <u>go</u> to the front desk to check-in. The receptionist <u>asks</u> them for their last names and for their picture identification cards. She <u>says</u>, "Thank you". She <u>gives</u> them keys to their rooms. Then she <u>shows</u> them the way to the second floor.

    The two couples <u>put</u> their bags in their rooms. Then they <u>go</u> down to the restaurant for breakfast. They <u>talk</u> about Delhi. They <u>decide</u> to see Mahatma Gandhi's Memorial.

2. Rose, Luke, Carol and Tom ***<u>will arrive</u>*** (arrive) at the Peace Hotel in Delhi. They ***<u>will go</u>*** (go) to the front desk to check-in. The receptionist ***<u>will ask</u>*** (ask) them for their last names and for their picture identification cards. She ***<u>will say</u>*** (say) "Thank you". She ***<u>will give</u>*** (give) them keys to their rooms. Then she ***<u>will show</u>*** (show) them the way to the second floor.

    The two couples ***<u>will put</u>*** (put) their bags in their rooms. Then they ***<u>will go</u>*** (go) down to the restaurant for breakfast. They ***<u>will talk</u>*** (talk) about Delhi. They ***<u>will decide</u>*** (decide) to see Mahatma Gandhi's Memorial.

Teachers Guide

Lesson 36 Continued

TEST 9 TOTAL MARKS: 50

ORAL QUESTIONS FOR TEST 9

	QUESTIONS	ANSWERS
1.	Were you wearing blue jeans yesterday?	Yes, I was wearing blue jeans yesterday. No, I wasn't wearing blue jeans yesterday
2.	What is the first month of the year?	January is the first month of the year.
3.	Were you hiking up a mountain yesterday?	Yes, I was hiking up a mountain yesterday. No, I wasn't hiking up a mountain yesterday.
4.	Will you see your friend tomorrow?	Yes, I will see my friend tomorrow. No, I won't see my friend tomorrow.
5.	Will you go to Delhi this year?	Yes, I will (I'll) go to Delhi this year. No, I will not (won't) go to Delhi this year.

ANSWERS TO THE WRITTEN QUESTIONS

6.	Did you drive a car to class?	Yes, I drove a car to class. No, I didn't drive a car to class.
7.	Will you see your friend next week?	Yes, I'll see my friend next week. No, I will not (won't) see my friend next week.
8.	Did you have breakfast this morning?	Yes, I had breakfast this morning. No, I didn't have (any) breakfast this morning.
9.	Did you buy some juice today?	Yes, I bought some juice today No, I didn't buy any juice today.
10.	Were you eating dinner at noon yesterday?	Yes, I was eating dinner at noon yesterday. No, I wasn't eating dinner at noon yesterday.

ANSWERS TO MATCH THE MEANING

a holiday	you don't work
a restaurant	you eat there
January	the first month of the year
music	you listen to it
blue jeans	you wear them

Teachers Guide

TEST 9   LESSONS 33 to 36   NAME: _____

Write the answers to the oral questions in sentences. (4 marks each)

1. _____
2. _____
3. _____
4. _____
5. _____

Answer these questions in sentences: (4 marks each)

6. Did you drive a car to class?

   _____

7. Will you see your friend next week?

   _____

8. Did you have breakfast this morning?

   _____

9. Did you buy some juice today?

   _____

10. Were you eating dinner at noon yesterday?

    _____

MATCH THE MEANING
Put the right meaning beside the words. (2 marks each)

11. a holiday   _____

12. a restaurant   _____

13. January   _____

14. music   _____

15. blue jeans   _____

you listen to it   the first month of the year   you don't work
you eat there   you wear them

Teachers Guide

Lesson 37

NOTE: **"Going to" is grammatically correct when talking about a plan made in the past.**
Last year I decided to learn English. I'm <u>going to</u> learn it.

"Will" is used to express willingness.
The phone is ringing. I will answer it.

**It is also used to talk about something that might happen in the future.
Both "will" and "going to" are used in general speech.
The above differences in use are not too important for students at this level.
In many cases either "will" or "going to" can be used.**

ORAL QUESTIONS

NOTE: The questions below that use "will" are requesting a willingness of someone to do something.

Are you going to buy a T-shirt? — *Yes, I'm going to buy a T-shirt.*
No, I'm not going to buy a T-shirt.

Will you help your friend? — *Yes, I'll help my friend.*
No, I won't help my friend.

Are you going to eat dinner at home? — *Yes, I'm going to eat dinner at home.*
No, I'm not going to eat dinner at home.

Are you going to see your teacher? — *Yes, I'm going to see my teacher.*
No, I'm not going to see my teacher.

Will you close the door, please? — *Yes, I'll close the door.*
No, I won't close the door.

Will you bring me a glass of juice, please? — *Yes, I'll bring you a glass of juice.*
No, I don't have any juice. / I won't…

Are you going to go to a party tonight? — *Yes, I'm going to go to a party tonight.*
No, I'm not going to go to a party tonight.

Are you going to wear blue jeans tomorrow? — *Yes, I'm going to wear blue jeans tomorrow.*
No, I'm not going to wear blue jeans tomorrow.

Are you going to meet your friend at 6 AM? — *Yes, I'm going to meet my friend at 6 AM.*
No, I'm not going to meet my friend at 6 AM.

Are you going to sleep all day tomorrow? — *Yes, I'm going to sleep all day tomorrow.*
No, I'm not going to sleep all day tomorrow.

Are you going to watch television tonight? — *Yes, I'm going to watch television tonight.*
No, I'm not going to watch television tonight.

Are you going to eat an apple today? — *Yes, I'm going to eat an apple today.*
No, I'm not going to eat an apple today.

Are you going to have a holiday tomorrow? — *Yes, I'm going to have a holiday tomorrow.*
No, I'm not going to have a holiday tomorrow.

Are you going to walk in the park on Saturday? — *Yes, I'm going to walk in the park on…*
No, I'm not going to walk in the park on…

Are you going to go to a nearby restaurant? — *Yes, I'm going to go to a nearby restaurant.*
No, I'm not going to go to a nearby restaurant.

Teachers Guide

Lesson 37 Continued

PAGE 80 **ANSWERS TO THE WORKBOOK QUESTIONS** **EXERCISE 1**

1. They go to the mountains. — *They are going to go to the mountains.*
2. They walk into the park. — *They are going to walk into the park.*
3. They drive to another city. — *They are going to drive to another city.*
4. He drinks mango juice. — *He is going to drink mango juice.*
5. He looks for his car. — *He is going to look for his car.*
6. She paints a picture. — *She is going to paint a picture.*
7. It will rain. — *It is going to rain.*
8. They listen to the radio. — *They are going to listen to the radio.*
9. They practice archery. — *They are going to practice archery.*
10. He walks to town. — *He is going to walk to town.*

PAGE 80 **POSSIBLE ANSWERS TO THE WORKBOOK QUESTIONS** **EXERCISE 2**

1. When / go — *When are you going to go?*
2. Where / live — *Where are you going to live?*
3. How / know — *How are you going to know?*
4. Who / meet — *Who are you going to meet?*
5. What / ask — *What are you going to ask?*

PAGE 81 **ANSWERS TO THE WORKBOOK QUESTIONS** **EXERCISE 3**

clock — *it tells the time*
brochure — *it tells about something*
garden — *a place with beautiful trees*
a plan — *it tells you what to do*
hotel — *you sleep and eat there*
desk — *you sit at it*

Teachers Guide

| Lesson 37 Continued |

PAGE 81   ANSWERS TO THE WORKBOOK QUESTIONS   **EXERCISE 4**

1. *Yes, I'm going to leave home at half past eight.*
   No, I'm not going to leave home at half past eight.

2. *Yes, I'm going to have tea with my friend at ten forty-five.*
   No, I'm not going to have tea with my friend at ten forty-five.

3. *Yes, I'm going to help my friend tomorrow.*
   No, I'm not going to help my friend tomorrow.

4. *Yes, I'm going to go to my friend's party at nine fifteen.*
   No, I'm not going to go to my friend's party at nine fifteen.

5. *Yes, I'm going to go to a church today.*
   No, I'm not going to go to a church today.

6. *Yes, I'm going to be at school tomorrow.*
   No, I'm not going to be at school tomorrow.

7. *I'm going to _____ after dinner.*
   I don't know what I'm going to do after dinner.

8. *Yes, I'm going to be hiking in the mountains next week.*
   No, I'm not going to be hiking in the mountains next week.

9. *Yes, I'm going to visit a big city next year.*
   No, I'm not going to visit a big city next year.

10. Yes, I'm going to bring some juice to the party.
    No, I'm not going to bring any juice to the party.

PAGE 135   GUIDE ACTIVITY

ACTIVITY 3   Cut the question and answers into cards and give them to the students.

Divide the students into two teams. They are to ask each other these questions.

Teachers Guide

Lesson 37 Continued

Are you going to come to class next week?
Yes, I'm going to come to class next week.
No, I'm not going to come to class next ...

Are you going to go swimming on the weekend?
Yes, I'm going to go swimming on the ...
No, I'm not going to go swimming on the ...

Are you going to buy a new dress tomorrow?
Yes, I'm going to buy a new dress tomorrow.
No, I'm not going to buy a new dress tomorrow.

Are you going to visit your friend next week?
Yes, I'm going to visit my friend next week.
No, I'm not going to visit my friend next week.

Are you going to eat supper at 6:00 PM?
Yes, I'm going to eat supper at 6:00 PM.
No, I'm not going to eat supper at 6:00 PM.

Are you going to go to the mountains tomorrow?
Yes, I'm going to go to the mountains tomorrow.
No, I'm not going to go to the mountains tomorrow.

Are you going to buy some juice today?
Yes, I'm going to buy some juice today.
No, I'm not going to buy any juice today.

Are you going to go to town next week?
Yes, I'm going to go to town next week.
No, I'm not going to go to town next week.

Is your father going to go to work tonight?
Yes, my father is going to go to work ...
No, my father is not going to go to work...

Is your family going to have a holiday this month?
Yes, my family is going to have a holiday ...
No, my family isn't going to have a holiday...

Are you going to wear a hat tonight?
Yes, I'm going to wear a hat tonight.
No, I'm not going to wear a hat tonight.

Are you going to have a holiday in January?
Yes, I'm going to have a holiday in January.
No, I'm not going to have a holiday in ...

Are you going to get home at midnight?
Yes, I'm going to get home at midnight.
No, I'm not going to get home at midnight.

Is it going to rain today?
Yes, it's going to rain today.
No, it's not going to rain today.

Are you going to have a party tomorrow?
Yes, I'm going to have a party tomorrow.
No, I'm not going to have a party tomorrow.

Are you going to need a car tomorrow?
Yes, I'm going to need a car tomorrow.
No, I'm not going to need a car tomorrow.

Teachers Guide

Lesson 38

ORAL QUESTIONS

What is your doctor's name? *My doctor's name is _____.*
Did you get married yesterday? *Yes, I got married yesterday.*
No, I didn't get married yesterday.

Are you an English student? *Yes, I'm an English student.*
Is your mother a homemaker? *Yes, my mother is a homemaker.*
No, my mother isn't a homemaker.

Continue asking these questions using: (some of the words are new)
secretary, store clerk, actress, nurse, lawyer, electrician, engineer, student.

How do you get to work/school? *I get to work by _____. (bicycle...)*
I get to work on _____. (foot ...)

Do you stay in a hotel when you travel? *Yes, I stay in a hotel.*
No, I don't stay in a hotel.
No, I stay with friends.

Is there a hospital in your city? *Yes, there is a hospital in my city.*
No, there isn't a hospital in my city.

Do you go to work/school by motorcycle? *Yes, I go by motorcycle.*
No, I don't go by motorcycle

Do you travel by bus? *Yes, I travel by bus.*
No, I don't travel by bus.

Continue asking the last two questions using:
on roller-blades, on horseback, on foot, by boat, by train, by plane

Will you travel by boat next summer? *Yes, I'll travel **by** boat next summer.*
*No, I won't travel **by** boat next summer.*

Do you go to town on foot? *Yes, I (usually) go to town **on** foot.*
*No, I don't go to town **on** foot.*

Do you travel on horseback sometimes? *Yes, I travel **on** horseback.*
*No, I don't travel **on** horseback.*

PAGE 82   **ANSWERS TO THE WORKBOOK QUESTIONS**   **EXERCISE 1**

1. I come to class by car / bus / train / on foot.
2. I get home by car / bus / train. I get home on foot. I walk home.
3. Yes, I am going to go to Bombay by plane. / No, I am not going to go to Bombay by plane.
4. Yes, I'm going to go to England by boat. / No, I am not going to go to England by boat.
5. Yes, I am going to go to work by bicycle. / No, I am not going to go to work by bicycle.
6. Yes, I am going to get married tomorrow. No, I am not going to get married tomorrow.

Note to the teacher:
The verb "to get" can be followed by an adjective or a past participle when it means <u>become</u>.
EXAMPLES: I get hungry.   I got married.   It is getting late.   They were getting sleepy.

Teachers Guide

Lesson 38 Continued

PAGE 82   ANSWERS TO THE WORKBOOK QUESTIONS   **EXERCISE 2**

Ruth went **to** town **at** 10:30 **on** Thursday. It was raining so she went **by** car. She had **to** meet her friend Nancy **at** noon. Nancy lives **on** Baker Street **in** another town. She came **by** train.

PAGE 82   ANSWERS TO THE WORKBOOK QUESTIONS   **EXERCISE 3**

1. I came to class on foot / by car / by bus.
2. I got to school / work by _____ two years ago.
3. Yes, I sometimes travel on skis. / No, I don't travel on skis.
4. I will get to town by bus / car / train / on foot.
5. A good way to travel is by / on _____.
6. Yes, I like to travel by bus. No, I don't like to travel by bus.

PAGE 83   ANSWERS TO THE WORKBOOK QUESTIONS   **EXERCISE 4**

1. **Did you come to class on skis?**
   Yes, __ came to class on skis.
   No, __ didn't come to class on skis.
2. **Do you go to work by train?**
   Yes, __ goes to work by train.
   No, __ doesn't go to work by train.
3. **Do you go to the Post Office on foot?**
   Yes, __ goes to the Post Office on foot.
   No, __ doesn't go to the Post Office on foot.
4. **Did you come to class by car?**
   Yes, __ came to class by car.
   No. __ didn't come to class by car.
5. **Did you go to another city by bus?**
   Yes, __ went to another city by bus.
   No, __ didn't go to another city by...
6. **Do you get home by taxi?**
   Yes, __ gets home by taxi.
   No, __ doesn't get home by taxi.
7. **Did you go to the hospital on horseback?**
   Yes, __ went to the hospital on horseback.
   No, __ didn't go to the hospital on horseback.
8. **Can you go to work by boat?**
   No, __ can't go to work by boat.

PAGE 83   ANSWERS TO THE WORKBOOK QUESTIONS   **EXERCISE 5**

Rose, Luke, Carol and Tom **are arriving** (arrive) at the Peace Hotel in Delhi. While they are standing at the front desk checking-in, the receptionist **is asking** (ask) them for their last names and for their picture identification cards. She says, "Thank you". After about five minutes she **is giving** (give) them the keys to their rooms and **is showing** (shows) them the way to the second floor.

The two couples put their bags in their rooms. Then they go down to the restaurant for breakfast. While they **are sitting** (sit) at a table they **are talking** (talk) about Delhi. They **are deciding** (decide) what they will do.

PAGE 84   ANSWERS TO THE BINGO GAME   **ACTIVITY 3**

12	gave	**1**	**wrote**	11	used	5	told
21	wore	15	cooked	7	answered	19	followed
18	worked	10	asked	16	returned	4	drank
20	wanted	3	rode	17	met	23	needed
6	started	22	happened	9	drove	8	attended
13	arrived	2	read	24	got	14	traveled

Teachers Guide

Lesson 39 - Review

Were you listening to the radio today?	Yes, I was listening to the radio today.
No, I wasn't listening to the radio today.

Is it raining now?	Yes, it's raining now
No, it isn't raining now.

Did you cook dinner yesterday?	Yes, I cooked dinner yesterday.
No, I didn't cook dinner yesterday.

Were you wearing a tie this morning?	Yes, I was wearing a tie this morning.
No, I wasn't wearing a tie this morning.

Were you driving a car today?	Yes, I was driving a car today.
No, I wasn't driving a car today.

Were you watching TV last night?	Yes, I was watching TV last night.
No, I wasn't watching TV last night.

Were you studying yesterday?	Yes, I was studying yesterday.
No, I wasn't studying yesterday.

Did you visit your friend last night?	Yes, I visited my friend last night.
No, I didn't visit my friend last night.

Do you eat supper at nine PM?	Yes, I eat supper at nine PM.
No, I don't eat supper at nine PM.

Were you playing basketball an hour ago?	Yes, I was playing basketball an hour ago.
No, I wasn't playing basketball an hour ago.

Do you live nearby?	Yes, I live nearby.
No, I don't live nearby.

Are you going to go swimming in January?	Yes, I'm going to go swimming in January.
No, I'm not going to go swimming in January.

Where do you wear your hat?	I wear my hat on my head.

Were you wearing jeans yesterday?	Yes, I was wearing jeans yesterday.
No, I wasn't wearing jeans yesterday.

Will you come to the party?	Yes, I'll come to the party.
No, I won't come to the party.

Were you riding an elephant today?	Yes, I was riding an elephant today.
No, I wasn't riding an elephant today.

Did you drink three cups of coffee today?	Yes, I drank three cups of coffee today.
No, I didn't drink three cups of coffee today.

Were you sleeping last night?	Yes, I was sleeping last night.
No, I wasn't sleeping last night.

Do you watch TV in the morning?	Yes, I watch TV in the morning.
No, I don't watch TV in the morning.

Does your friend have a birthday today?	Yes, my friend has a birthday today.
No, my friend doesn't have a birthday today.

Does your friend speak English?	Yes, my friend speaks English.
No, my friend doesn't speak English.

Teachers Guide

Lesson 39 Continued

ANSWERS TO THE WORKBOOK QUESTIONS

PAGE 85 — **EXERCISE 1**

1. Yes, I was eating lunch at eleven o'clock. / No, I wasn't eating lunch at eleven o'clock.
2. Yes, I walk outside in the morning. / No, I don't walk outside in the morning.
3. I was with my friend last night. / I was at home/at the movies/in town last night.
4. Yes, my teacher is laughing now. / No, my teacher isn't laughing now.
5. Yes, I was writing a letter on the weekend. / No, I wasn't writing a letter on the weekend.
6. Yes, I was living in San Francisco last year. / No, I wasn't living in San Francisco last year.
7. I wear my hat on my head.
8. Yes, I usually listen to the radio on Sundays. / No, I don't usually listen to the radio on...
9. Yes, I was wearing a T-shirt this morning. / No, I wasn't wearing a T-shirt this morning.
10. Yes, it's going to rain. / No, it isn't going to rain.
11. Yes, I was sleeping at eight o'clock last night. / No, I wasn't sleeping at eight o'clock last...
12. Yes, I was walking in the park on the weekend. / No, I wasn't walking in the park on the weekend.

ANSWERS TO THE STUDENT BOOK QUESTIONS

PAGE 69 — **ACTIVITY 1**

She is a **_nurse_**.   He is a **_taxi driver._**
He is an **_artist_**.   He is a **_mechanic_**.
He is a **_policeman_**.   He is a **_teacher_**.

ACTIVITY 3: Make **one copy** of the chart below and give **one name to each student.**
The students are meeting friends that they haven't seen for a long time.
Put this example on the blackboard.

FIRST SPEAKER: Hello / Hi _____. How are you doing?
SECOND SPEAKER: I'm _____. How are you?
FIRST SPEAKER: I'm _____. Are you living here now?
SECOND SPEAKER: Yes, I like it here. / No, I'm living in _____.
FIRST SPEAKER: It's good to see you. Let's have a / coffee / lemonade.
SECOND SPEAKER: Great. Let's go.

ANNE I'm fine. Bombay	RICHARD Very well, thanks Delhi	SARAH I'm so-so Vancouver	RUTH Just great! Ottawa
CAMILLE Not so good. New York	ALEXANDER I'm not very well. Paris	BRUCE I'm doing fine. Mexico City	CAROL I'm okay. Lisbon
SUSAN Not badly. London	MARIA I'm fine. Rome	PAUL I am fine, thanks. San Francisco	DAVID I'm not so good. Toronto
KATE I'm so-so. Hong Kong	HELEN Not badly. Frankfurt	ROBERT I'm okay. Madrid	MARK Very well, thanks. Prague

Teachers Guide

ACTIVITY 2

Lesson 39 Continued

NAME: Deborah Mills
HOW ARE YOU? I'm fine, thanks.
MARITAL STATUS: single
HOBBIES: basketball
OCCUPATION: teacher
GET-UP TIME: seven ten
FAVORITE DRINK: juice
SATURDAYS: I'm going to see my friend.
LAST HOLIDAY: 6 weeks ago

NAME: Brooke Patterson
HOW ARE YOU? I'm not very well.
MARITAL STATUS: single
HOBBIES: roller-blades
OCCUPATION: actress
GET-UP TIME: six fifteen
FAVORITE DRINK: water
SATURDAYS: I'm going to go to town.
LAST HOLIDAY: five years ago

NAME: Lynn Nash
HOW ARE YOU? I'm okay.
MARITAL STATUS: married
HOBBIES: reading
OCCUPATION: doctor
GET-UP TIME: half past six
FAVORITE DRINK: Coke
SATURDAYS: I'm going to go swimming.
LAST HOLIDAY: four days ago

NAME: Adrian (Adrienne) May
HOW ARE YOU? Just great!
MARITAL STATUS: married
HOBBIES: theater
OCCUPATION: carpet maker
GET-UP TIME: a quarter to eight
FAVORITE DRINK: coffee
SATURDAYS: I'm going to play volleyball
LAST HOLIDAY: last February

NAME: Bruce Robertson
HOW ARE YOU? I'm so-so.
MARITAL STATUS: single
HOBBIES: bicycling (cycling)
OCCUPATION: policeman
GET-UP TIME: twenty past nine
FAVORITE DRINK: juice
SATURDAYS: I'm going to go to the park.
LAST HOLIDAY: last March

NAME: Penny Cuthbert
HOW ARE YOU? I'm doing well.
MARITAL STATUS: married
HOBBIES: writing
OCCUPATION: nurse
GET-UP TIME: twelve noon
FAVORITE DRINK: lemonade
SATURDAYS: I'm going to go to the library.
LAST HOLIDAY: last July

NAME: Alan Dunning
HOW ARE YOU? I'm fine, thanks.
MARITAL STATUS: single
HOBBIES: soccer
OCCUPATION: artist
GET-UP TIME: twenty to eight
FAVORITE DRINK: juice
SATURDAYS: I'm going to have a holiday.
LAST HOLIDAY: a year and a half ago

NAME: Elizabeth Fraser
HOW ARE YOU? I'm not so good..
MARITAL STATUS: married
HOBBIES: dancing
OCCUPATION: homemaker
GET-UP TIME: a quarter to nine
FAVORITE DRINK: coffee
SATURDAYS: I'm going to go to the theater.
LAST HOLIDAY: six months ago

Lesson 39 Continued

NAME: Miranda Bates
HOW ARE YOU? I'm doing fine.
MARITAL STATUS: single
HOBBIES: computers
OCCUPATION: teacher
GET-UP TIME: seven thirty
FAVORITE DRINK: Sprite
SATURDAYS: I'm going to visit my friends.
LAST HOLIDAY: last June

NAME: Daniela Black
HOW ARE YOU? I'm okay
MARITAL STATUS: single
HOBBIES: cooking
OCCUPATION: nurse
GET-UP TIME: five forty-five
FAVORITE DRINK: coffee
SATURDAYS: I'm going to see my friend.
LAST HOLIDAY: a week and a half ago

NAME: Winston Donovan
HOW ARE YOU? Just great!
MARITAL STATUS: single
HOBBIES: swimming
OCCUPATION: wood carver
GET-UP TIME: seven fifteen
FAVORITE DRINK: coffee
SATURDAYS: I'm going to play soccer.
LAST HOLIDAY: the day before yesterday

NAME: Sally Ray
HOW ARE YOU? I'm so-so.
MARITAL STATUS: married
HOBBIES: volleyball
OCCUPATION: doctor
GET-UP TIME: six forty-five
FAVORITE DRINK: Coke
SATURDAYS: I'm going to be at home.
LAST HOLIDAY: last week

NAME: Linda Watts
HOW ARE YOU? I'm fine, thanks.
MARITAL STATUS: single
HOBBIES: roller-blading
OCCUPATION: homemaker
GET-UP TIME: six o'clock
FAVORITE DRINK: Coke
SATURDAYS: I'm going to go to town.
LAST HOLIDAY: last September

NAME: Margaret Selkirk
HOW ARE YOU? I'm not so good.
MARITAL STATUS: married
HOBBIES: traveling
OCCUPATION: nurse
GET-UP TIME: nine thirty
FAVORITE DRINK: juice
SATURDAYS: I'm going to read a book.
LAST HOLIDAY: last April

NAME: Joseph Woods
HOW ARE YOU? Just great!
MARITAL STATUS: single
HOBBIES: theater
OCCUPATION: taxi driver
GET-UP TIME: eleven fifteen
FAVORITE DRINK: juice
SATURDAYS: I'm going to listen to music.
LAST HOLIDAY: two weeks ago

NAME: Samuel Munn
HOW ARE YOU? I'm so-so.
MARITAL STATUS: single
HOBBIES: music
OCCUPATION: student
GET-UP TIME: seven o'clock
FAVORITE DRINK: lemonade
SATURDAYS: I'm going to study.
LAST HOLIDAY: six months ago

Teachers Guide

LESSON 40 - FINAL TEST

Notes to the teacher:
The philosophy of Learning English Curriculum is to give the students the best possible conditions for doing well on each test.
The test questions cover the work that has been introduced.

When marking the test, subtract one mark for each mistake.
Do not subtract marks for spelling.
If the student doesn't understand any of the meaning of the question, then no marks are given.
If there is some understanding then give them some marks.
Before starting the test, take 10 minutes to ask some of the oral questions in Lesson 39.
This will help the students to start thinking in English.

FINAL TEST TOTAL MARKS: 100

ORAL QUESTIONS AND ANSWERS FOR THE FINAL TEST

The students are to write the answers to these oral questions in sentences.
Note: The words in (brackets are other possible answers to the questions.

	QUESTIONS	ANSWERS
1.	How are you today?	I'm (I am) fine. (thanks / thank you)
2.	Do you live in France?	Yes, I live in France.
		No, I don't live in France.
3.	How many English classes do you have each week?	I have _____ English classes each week.
4.	Did you buy some chicken today?	Yes, I bought some chicken today.
		No, I didn't buy any chicken today.
5.	Were you in town yesterday?	Yes, I was in town yesterday.
		No, I wasn't (was not) in town yesterday.
6.	What are you doing now?	I'm writing (a test) now.
7.	When are you going to phone your friend?	I'm going to phone my friend on/at _____.
8.	Does your friend have a dog?	Yes, my friend has a dog.
		No, my friend doesn't (does not) have a dog.
9.	Will you help your friend tonight?	Yes, I'll (I will) help my friend tonight.
		No, I won't help my friend tonight.
		No, I won't be able to help my friend tonight.
10.	Is it raining now?	Yes, it's (it is) raining now.
		No, it isn't (is not) raining now.

Teachers Guide

FINAL TEST   NAME:_____

Answer the questions in sentences: (4 marks each)

1. _____
2. _____
3. _____
4. _____
5. _____
6. _____
7. _____
8. _____
9. _____
10. _____

Use these words to complete the sentences: (2 marks each)

   to   in   at   in front of   on

Craig and Jessica walked (11) _____ town to meet their friends (12) _____ _____ _____ the restaurant (13) _____ 7:00 (14) _____ the evening. When their friends arrived they sat (15) _____ a table, and ordered pizza. After dinner they went (16) _____ the theater (17) _____ Market Street. On Sunday afternoon they went (18) _____ the park.

Put these words into sentences. (4 marks each)

19. a, She, reading, book, is   _____
20. man, in, store, volunteers, The, a   _____
21. are, Canada, They, from   _____

Teachers Guide

145

FINAL TEST CONTINUED   NAME: _____

Answer these questions in sentences. (4 marks each)

22. Do some of the men have hats?
_____

23. Where are the men?
_____

24. How many fish do they have?
_____

25. Are the men wearing jackets?
_____

26. Are they sitting in the boat?
_____

27. Are you going to go fishing
_____

28. What is grandfather doing?
_____

29. Do you drink juice?
_____

Now you can have juice, too!

Teachers Guide

FINAL TEST ANSWERS CONTINUED

Use these words to complete the sentences: (2 marks each)

| to | in | at | in front of | on |

Craig and Jessica walked (11) *to* town to meet their friends (12) *in front of* the restaurant (13) *at* 7:00 (14) *in* the evening. When their friends arrived they sat (15) *at* a table, and ordered pizza. After dinner they went (16) *to* the theater (17) *on* Market Street. On Sunday afternoon they went (18) *to* the park.

Put these words into sentences. (4 marks each)

19. a, She, reading, book, is — *She is reading a book.*
20. man, in, store, volunteers, The, a — *The man volunteers in a store.*
21. are, Canada, They, from — *They are from Canada.*

Answer these questions in sentences. (4 marks each)

22. Do some of the men have hats? — *Yes, some of the men have hats.*
23. Where are the men? — *The men are in the boat.*
24. How many fish do they have? — *They have three fish.*
25. Are the men wearing jackets? — *No, the men aren't wearing jackets.* / *No, the men are not wearing jackets.*
26. Are they sitting in the boat? — *No, they aren't (are not) sitting in the boat.*
27. Are you going to go fishing? — *Yes, I'm (I am) going to go fishing.* / *No, I'm not going to go fishing.*
28. What is grandfather doing? — *Grandfather is drinking.*
29. Do you drink juice? — *Yes, I drink juice.* / *No, I don't drink juice.*

Teachers Guide

About Learning English Curriculum Ltd.

Learning English Curriculum began in Czechoslovakia in 1990. Shortly after the Velvet Revolution that freed the country of Communism. The authors began writing these lessons as they taught English to their Czech Students at the English Centre in Karlovy Vary. The students played a vital role in the development of this series. The authors consulted with them by having them complete student surveys wherein they rated the extensive variety of activities and lessons that they had participated in. Discussion of the results followed and any item that was rated below 8, on a scale of 1 to 10, was discarded. Thus, Learning English Curriculum evolved through consultation with our English second language students.

Since 20095 thousands of people around the world have visited our web sites. At this time purchases of our Teen-Adult Curriculum, Children's Curriculum, Children's Storybooks and our listening programs have been made from more than 100 countries.

At Learning English Curriculum, we have a suggestion regarding the printing of our books in an economical and environmentally friendly way. It is our experience that when students begin something new there are always those that, for a number of reasons, don't continue. In order to cut expenses and avoid wasting paper, we suggest that you begin the classes by providing only the first lessons of the printed book. These small things do make a difference.

Customization of your covers

You may be interested in the customization of your covers. (White Label Services
This personalizes your textbooks and makes them a visible part of your school's curriculum. For this service contact us at: info@efl-esl.com

Members of our team with professional degrees have combined years of teaching experience and editing to produce these teaching materials.

Team Members for this publication:
Editors:
Daisy A. Stocker B.Ed., .Ed.
Dr. George A. Stocker D.D.S.

Contributor:
Brian Stocker MA

Visit us Online for More

https://www.efl-esl.com

BEGINNERS LESSON PLANS BOOK 1

20 complete lesson plans
3 Textbooks plus
Downloadable Audio and Video

Includes:

- Student Reader
- Student Workbook
- Teachers Guide
- 20 lessons
- 5 tests
- 4 reviews
- Glossary
- Download PDF or Paperback

Book 1 Overview

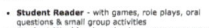
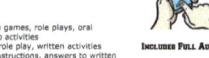

BEGINNERS LESSON PLANS BOOK 2

20 complete lesson plans
3 Textbooks plus
Downloadable Audio and Video

Includes:

- Student Reader
- Student Workbook
- Teachers Guide
- 20 lessons
- 5 tests
- 4 reviews
- Glossary
- Download PDF or Paperback

Book 2 Overview

Listening and Speaking Workbook

Complete Listening and Speaking English Workbook – includes full downloadable audio!

- Vocabulary for each Lesson
- Everyday Conversations – Listen to full audio then role-play!
- 14 Lessons
- 2 Review Chapters
- 2 Full Audio Tests with Answer Key
- Role Play
- Telephone Conversations and role play
- Question and Answer Dialogues

https://efl-esl.com/listening-speaking-english/

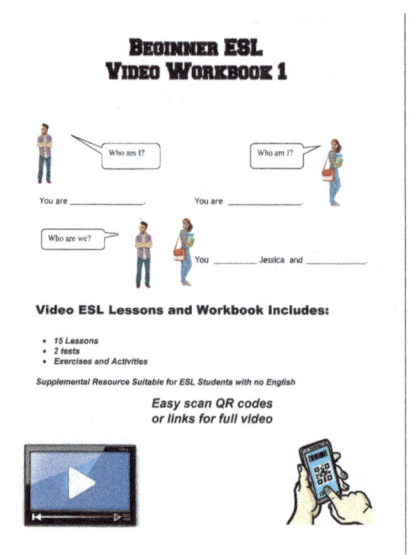

Beginners ESL Video Workbook

Includes:

- 15 lesson plans with full video
- Supplemental activities and games
- Video introduction for all topics

Learn More https://efl-esl.com/video-workbooks/

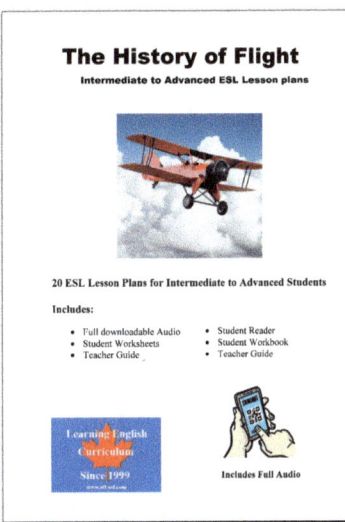

Intermediate to Advanced ESL Lesson Plans for Adults

From the Ancient Greeks to Leonardo Da Vinci's flying machines, to Orville and Wilbur Wright, to WWII flying Ace, the Red Baron, to modern day space travel!

Includes:

- **Full audio**
- 20 Lessons – 40 hours of classroom time!
- Print as many Copies as Required!
- Teacher's guide
- Student Reader
- Student Workbook
- Complete instructions — ready for the classroom
- No preparation

https://efl-esl.com/curriculum/flight/

Children's ESL

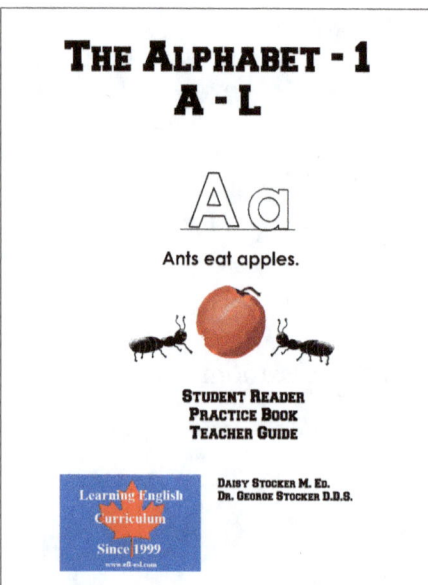

This book introduces the alphabet from A to L and the numbers from 1 – 10.

Includes:

- Student book – 37 pages
- Student Workbook – 24 pages
- Teacher's Guide Book – 50 pages
- Glossary — 142 new words
- Colorful games and activities suitable for lamination – use over and over!

https://efl-esl.com/alphabet-activities-for-esl-students/

ESL Graphic Novels for Kids (Comic Books)

These books offer an oral approach for young ESL / EFL students aged 6 - 10.

They contain high interest stories, written in the graphics novel format that children love. This is very suitable for supplementary study, home school, as well as for summer camps.

https://efl-esl.com/esl-graphic-novels-for-children/

www.ingramcontent.com/pod-product-compliance
Lightning Source LLC
LaVergne TN
LVHW080249260326
834688LV00042BA/1193